The story of
Venus

Andrew Dalby

THE BRITISH MUSEUM PRESS

Also by Andrew Dalby and available from The British Museum Press
The Story of Bacchus
Dangerous Tastes: The Story of Spices
The Classical Cookbook (with Sally Grainger)

Copyright © 2005 Andrew Dalby

Andrew Dalby has asserted his moral right to be identified as the author of this work

First published in 2005 by The British Museum Press
A division of The British Museum Company Ltd
38 Russell Square, London WC1B 3QQ

A catalogue record for this book is available from the British Library

ISBN-13: 978-0-7141-2243-4

ISBN-10: 0-7141-2243-2

Designed by Chloë Alexander
Typeset in New Caledonia and Bliss
Printed in Spain by Mateu Cromo, S.A. Pinto (Madrid)

Contents

1
The Birth of Venus 9

2
Marriage and Adultery 21

3
The Children of Venus 43

4
The Story of Adonis 63

5
The Events on Mount Ida 81

6
The Fall of Troy and the Origin of Rome 101

7
The Goddess of Love 115

Life Notes 129
Sources 135
Further Reading 149
Index 153

1

The Birth of Venus

A PHRODITE – VENUS, AS WE SHALL CALL HER BY HER ROMAN NAME – WAS born from the sea. Many writers call her 'the foam-born', and many images depict her rising from the waves. Full-grown, shapely, desirable, with one hand she wrings her long, wavy hair that is still wet from the waters of her mother's womb. With the other she pretends to conceal the secret places of her body. She stands on a scallop-shell as perfect and beautiful as herself.

The sea, therefore, was her mother. But Greek and Roman religion personified the inanimate world and the forces of nature: it was not enough to say 'the sea'. Since none of the well-known goddesses had accepted the responsibility of mothering Venus, the task was given retrospectively by the storytellers to a certain Dione, a shadowy divinity. Dione was possibly an Oceanid nymph, one of the daughters of Ocean who flows continually like a river all around the known world. Or perhaps she was a Nereid, a sea-nymph, daughter of Nereus and Doris. Or perhaps, placing her closer to the origin of all the gods and goddesses, Dione was one of the Titans, monstrous children of Ouranos, the Sky, and of Gaia, the Earth. In that case there must have been thirteen Titans, not twelve as is usually said.

There is, at all events, some agreement about one half of Venus's parentage. But a goddess must have a father, surely? If Venus rose fully formed from the sea, the child of Dione, then some male deity must have produced the seed that germinated in Dione's womb.

One might easily leap to the conclusion that Zeus, father of gods and men, well known for his brief sexual affairs with goddesses and women, had on some unknown occasion slept with Dione, had made her pregnant, and thus became the father of Venus. It seemed an easy solution, and some ancient poets accepted it; but it brought a problem with it. The sexual act, the act of procreation performed by humans and animals, the act that lovers consider to be the culmination of their elaborate courtship rituals, is the very thing over which Venus herself presides. It is her work. How can she herself be the product of it? Who, if not Venus, could have presided over the illicit pleasures of Zeus and Dione? One philosopher found an independent answer to this problem. Epimenides, an early Greek sage, taught his followers that Venus was the daughter of Kronos, father of Zeus, in the generation before the Olympians, at that distant time when the gods were of unfamiliar shape and their couplings took a form unimaginable by us. This parentage made Venus the sibling of the Moirai or Fates (who weave the threads of human life) and the Erinyes or Furies (who punish those guilty of unnatural crimes). It was indeed the mark of an ascetic philosopher to liken the activities of the Fates and Furies to those of Venus, equally capable on occasion of driving mortals to madness and destruction.

Epimenides' answer was not the most popular one. Eventually it was agreed that the origin of Venus was one generation earlier still. It happened in this way. Gaia, the Earth, who lay beneath, impregnated by Ouranos, the Sky, who lay above her, was the mother of many strange things. She brought forth the Titans, named above, and Okeanos the Ocean, and Pontos the Deep Sea, and the giant Kyklopes with one eye each in the middle of their foreheads, and the hundred-handed monsters Kottos and Briareos and Gyes. They were all fearsome creatures. Their father Ouranos disliked them and by his continual demand for intercourse prevented them even from emerging from their mother's womb. Now the most fearsome of the Titans, the wiliest of all, was Kronos.

Their mother, outraged by Ouranos's unending lust and unnatural hatred for his own children, produced a sharp flint with a sickle-shaped edge, and offered it to each of them in turn. None dared to say a word except Kronos. He spoke up bravely:

'I can feel no respect for our father, who has set us an example of wickedness. Very well, Mother: I will do this thing.'

So Gaia hid her son in an ambush, somewhere in a recess of her own vast body. When Ouranos came, as dark as night, to lie luxuriantly upon Gaia as he always did, Kronos reached out, grasped his father's testicles in his left hand and sliced them off with a swift movement of the flint sickle in his right. He threw them away behind him. Wherever the drops of blood fell on the surface of Gaia, each drop became a new child: this was the origin of the fierce Gigantes or Giants, and the Furies – which means that these were not the offspring of Kronos, as Epimenides claimed – and the goddesses who are called Meliai, the nymphs of the ash tree. But the testicles themselves fell into the sea far away. They floated for a long time, perhaps for hundreds of years, and a white foam (*aphros*) gathered about them, the last remnants of the seed of Ouranos.

In this foam, as it floated off the beautiful island of Kythera, to the south of the Greek mainland, a young woman was born. That is the reason, so it was said, why she was often given the title *Kythereia* in later times. But she was not yet fully formed, and she did not rise from the sea until the waves had carried her to Cyprus, to the shore where afterwards the city of Paphos would rise. Here she stepped ashore, and grass and flowers grew beneath her tender feet as she walked. This, the Greeks said, is why they often called her *Kypris* and *Kyprogenes*, the lady of Cyprus.

This was the origin of the goddess of love. Her own name in Greek was *Aphrodite*, and the Greeks were sure that this was because she was born from foam.

The ancient love goddess has many origins and many histories. The Minoans of Crete pictured her as a beautiful young woman, wearing a full skirt and a tight low-cut bodice that displays her perfect breasts. In one icon she brandishes a snake in either hand. Like Venus, she came from the sea; sea-shells in great numbers were offered at her shrines, and sometimes she was depicted blowing a triton-shell.

The Sumerians, who created the most ancient civilization of southern Mesopotamia, called their love goddess Inanna. *In the first days, when everything needful was brought into being*, and not long after Sky had moved away from Earth, an oak sapling began to grow by the banks of the Euphrates, or so the Sumerians said. The waters nourished it, but the south wind tore at its branches and loosened its roots and so the river swept it away. A beautiful young woman, daughter of the Moon, came that way and pulled the tree out of the river. 'I shall plant this tree in my garden,' she said, 'and then, in due time, I shall have a chair and a bed.' She held it upright with her hands and firmed the soil around it with her feet. This woman was Inanna. She nurtured the tree until it became big and strong, and from it her brother Gilgamesh, legendary king of Erech, carved a chair and a bed for her.

One day she leaned against an apple tree in her garden. She considered her own naked body, and knew that with its persuasive power she could make men do whatever she wanted. So she put on the crown of the land between the rivers, a circlet of gold and lapis lazuli, and went to visit father Enki, the god of wisdom. They drank beer together until Enki was very drunk, and then, careless of the consequences, he raised his cup and formally presented to her seven of the *me*, the tablets of destiny, jealously guarded by him until that moment. They contained the special science with which she would rule men and animals ever afterwards, the science of sexual love. To each gift as he offered it Inanna replied, 'I accept.' That, according to the Sumerians, is how the beautiful young woman Inanna became the goddess of love and the queen of Heaven; that is how love became important in the world. Afterwards, too late, Enki returned to sobriety and realized what he had done.

Venus, at any rate, first stood on earth at Paphos, in Cyprus. The Romans accepted the stories of Aphrodite as stories of their own goddess Venus. Roman poets often called her *Cytherea*, *Cypris* and *Paphia*, in reminiscence of her Eastern origins, and because these names will all fit easily into lines of Latin verse.

Was Eros in attendance at her birth? Hesiod said so in his *Theogony*, because Hesiod thought that Eros was an ancient god, one of the first and most powerful. Most later Greeks disagreed, believing, instead, that Eros was Venus's own son. We shall soon meet him in that role. On the other hand, Hesiod believed that the Horai were not yet born when Venus emerged from the sea; but others felt sure that it was these two goddesses, children of Zeus, who were at hand to attend her. Dressed in their golden veils, they gathered round and led her to the sanctuary that would ever afterwards be her favourite retreat.

These Horai are the 'Hours', if we are to translate their name literally, but that does not quite explain why they were the ideal attendants for Venus. We might rather call them the two 'Seasons' (and there were originally two, not four): in Greek the word *hora* means season also, and particularly the season at which plants and animals come to full ripeness. If a fruit is *horaios* it is ripe and ready for eating. If boys and girls are *horaioi* they are of an age for sexual love. Venus was born from the sea already fully formed, ready for adult life; thus it was natural that she should be adorned by the two Horai.

On her immortal head they placed a beautiful, finely woven golden wreath; to her pierced earlobes they attached earrings of costly gold and bronze; they draped jewelled necklaces around her tender neck that would sparkle on her silver-white breast – just such jewels as the Horai themselves are accustomed to wear when they go to the house of their father Zeus to join the wondrous dances of the immortals. Around her upper body, crossing *en sautoir* between her breasts, she wore an embroidered and pearl-studded band known to devotees as the *kestos himas*, a magical thing which drew to her all men who came within its power, and a possession that Venus is found by her modern devotees to have appropriated from Ishtar, Inanna and other ancient goddesses of love.

So, when they had adorned every part of her body, they led her in procession to present her to the gods and goddesses. The Greeks said that doves and sparrows pulled the chariot on which she rose to Mount

Olympos, doves because they are always kissing, sparrows because they are always procreating. The Romans imagined her riding on a swan or in a chariot drawn by swans, because, like some humans under the influence of Venus, swans mate for life and pine when their mate dies.

In whatever way she reached Olympos, its immortal inhabitants stretched out their hands in greeting and welcomed her joyfully. Every male among the gods desired Venus. Each of them hoped to be the one who would make her his wife and lead her to his own house.

On Mount Olympos, as Venus discovered that evening, the gods and goddesses dine together as one united family.

There are two circles. Hera, unless she is feeling particularly angry about something, will be there to preside over the ladies. Theirs is a quiet group, for Hestia, the goddess of the hearth, a homely figure, says very little. Grandmother Rhea sits opposite Hestia. She is the sister and wife of Kronos, who, hundreds of years ago, by cutting off his father's testicles, had caused Venus to be born; but now Kronos himself has been defeated and deposed by his son Zeus, husband and brother of Hera. Kronos is confined to Tartaros, the depth of the Underworld. Rhea, though she did not follow him into captivity, nowadays keeps silent, deferring to her daughter, white-armed Hera.

If Hera remains in her room, Demeter, a calm, motherly, somewhat sad figure, takes charge (not that the goddesses are unruly at dinner). Demeter is large and comfortable and always enveloped in a voluminous gown – an Earth Mother figure.

Athene and Artemis, the two youngest, are none too talkative. Both are beautiful, though with the slightly forbidding beauty of those who are dedicated to virginity.

Artemis, twin sister of Apollo, daughter of Zeus and goddess of the hunt, often has no time to change for dinner after a long day's chase. She tosses her bow and quiver into the corner and throws herself on to her couch, a little sweaty perhaps, her perfect skin glowing from its contact with the cool air of Earth, the red border of her short tunic flapping provocatively about her thighs. She knows perfectly well that her brothers and half-brothers, and even her uncle Poseidon, reclining in the other circle, will be unable wholly to avert their eyes as she makes her dramatic entrance. She doesn't mind at all. She is happy for it to be known that one or two mortals have been tempted to go further and to spy on her as she bathes in a woodland pool. The penalty for such spying is death.

Athene, unlike Artemis, does not dress for effect. She is a warrior goddess, and if she has to fight – even against the war god Ares – she always wins. But she is also the most intelligent of the immortals and prefers to solve problems without fighting. Her flashing golden helmet and bronze spear are never seen in the dining room. Nor is the famous *aigis*, the goatskin that she wears across her breast.

The victuals on Mount Olympos are of a special kind. The drink there is not wine but nectar; the food is ambrosia, food of the immortals – even their horses feed on ambrosia, according to the poet who composed the *Iliad*. The food is excellent, therefore, but unfortunately it is always the same. By the time the third course was being served, on her first evening at dinner on Olympos, Venus had realized that there was no need to bother to look at it. Instead there was always plenty of time for the gods to steal glances at the circle of goddesses and for the goddesses to look across brazenly at the circle of gods.

The gods have no need to dress for dinner. Zeus, who always takes the place of honour among them, reclines majestically. A robe, thrown nonchalantly across one shoulder, reveals his manly chest. The thunderbolt with which he is always armed when he poses for a portrait is put aside before he enters the dining room. He is a regal but at the same time touchy host, inclined to be querulous about the nectar and ambrosia but to take offence when others complain.

Zeus's brother Poseidon does not always dine in: he has his own palace under the sea, where his wife, the sea-goddess Amphitrite, daughter of Nereus, lives. If he is present, there will be loud talking and occasionally the raising of voices in anger as he and his brother score conversational points off one another.

Apollo is Zeus's most handsome son. His hair is golden, poets say, though painters usually make it dark because golden hair does not suit Greek features. He is musical, too, and is the soloist when the nine Muses entertain the immortals with song and music after dinner. He seems to have all the advantages – coupled with the gift of prophecy, for he presides over the oracle at Delphi, the centre of Greece and the centre of the world, where mortals go in hope of learning their future. Yet for some reason he is not at ease with the opposite sex.

Venus watched him as he told his companions, evidently not for the first time, of the musical competition to which he had invited Marsyas.

'… so I finally challenged him to play and sing at the same time. He had a flute, poor man, so he couldn't manage it! It was easy with a lyre. So the Muses had to award me the first prize. Do you know what I did?'

'I do, in fact,' Hermes began, but Apollo ran on regardless.

'I flayed him alive. It was a lengthy task, and he must have found it a very painful death. I saved the skin and hung it from a pine tree beside a spring. The river that flows from it …'

'… is called Marsyas,' said Hermes flatly.

'You must always stop me if I've told you a story before,' said Apollo in an irritated tone. 'I hate to bore people. I wonder if I've ever mentioned a nymph called Dryope …'

Young Hermes, son of Zeus and the nymph Maia, a thieving youngster who became the messenger of Mount Olympos, has dark hair, dark eyes and a boyish charm. He has had many affairs and many children. Venus watched him as he smiled and nodded at Apollo's story, arching his eyebrows at Poseidon, who did the same in return. It was obvious that they had already heard this story too. But Venus had not, and she listened a little more.

'… and then I turned into a snake, and I hissed, ssss! and all her friends ran away. So then of course I had her on her own and I could do whatever I wanted with her. So first of all …'

Venus's attention wandered from Apollo's reminiscences. Her thoughts were following a more serious path. She knew already that it would be her special privilege as goddess to give to men and women the gift of sexual love, with all the things that they would do together in the name of love. She began to imagine what some of those things would be.

Momentarily she was aware of Poseidon and Hermes laughing rudely at some detail of Apollo's story. Their heads were close together. Then Poseidon looked across straight at her for a moment, and said something under his breath to the others.

Her gifts, she decided there and then, were to be shared between two people only, and not afterwards told to others at a dinner party. She would punish those who betrayed lovers' secrets. Perhaps, in any case, she would not give her gift to Apollo. What about Poseidon? Well, after all, he had been led to say whatever he had said about her by Apollo's story. He looked strong, angry, passionate. Perhaps she and Poseidon could still be friends.

Ares, proud son of Zeus and Hera, sometimes arrives late for dinner, as does Artemis. He is often busy stirring up wars. He revels in the death and bloodshed that they bring. This evening, as it happened, he entered at an ideal moment. Venus had just realized that the third course of ambrosia was very much like the second, and had looked up again to see what else was happening. Their eyes met.

'My son Ares, late as usual,' his mother commented. 'You were introduced this morning, weren't you?'

'No,' said Venus at once, 'I'm sure we weren't.'

Ares had paused before joining the circle of gods. Venus was pleasantly aware of the perfect curve of her hip as she reclined beside Hera. She felt sure that Ares would notice it.

'He's not a bad boy at heart,' Hera continued, 'though he tends to come home dirty. Ares!' she called, in a voice that expected obedience, 'remember your manners. Come and be introduced. Where were you this morning? There's blood on your tunic. This is young Venus ... no, my dear, there's absolutely no need to get up for him if he arrives half way through dinner. Just give him your hand to kiss.'

'I was out early today, Mother,' said Ares. 'I have a war on just now among the Ethiopians. Venus: what a beautiful name.' He bowed low to kiss her hand and their eyes met again. 'We must have a talk tomorrow.'

'I'd like that,' Venus said lightly, and she turned to ask Artemis a question that suddenly occurred to her, allowing her right leg to stretch languidly as she shifted position.

Ares noticed that too.

2

Marriage and Adultery

THE UGLIEST AND MOST MISSHAPEN OF THE GODS WAS HEPHAISTOS. Hera had given birth to him without a father, some said; or else he was the child of the illicit sexual play between the young Hera and Zeus when they were only brother and sister, long before their marriage made them king and queen of the gods. At any rate, this first baby of Hera's seemed to have a crooked foot, and after a quick glance at him she threw him out of Olympos.

'My own child, Hephaistos, was the runt among all the immortal gods:' so said Hera herself in the course of later recriminations. 'His legs were shrivelled. I snatched him up in my hands and threw him down into the deep sea ...'

The sea-goddess Thetis in her silver sandals had caught him as he fell.

'... that bitch!' Hera finished angrily.

Hephaistos was also able to recall the occasion. Gods – even baby gods – know everything. His memories were somewhat different.

'Thetis is a goddess whom I honour,' he said. 'I was in great pain after I fell from the Sky – the act of my own shameless mother, who wanted to hide me from all others' sight because I was crippled – and Thetis saved me. I would have suffered dreadfully had I not been rescued by Thetis and her companion Eurynome, daughter of Ocean. I lived with them for nine years, making jewellery in abundance – brooches and curved bracelets, earrings and necklaces – down in their cave under the sea, surrounded by the foam and roar of Ocean. No one else knew of it, no gods or goddesses, no mortals, only the two of them.'

Hephaistos was always conscious of his gratitude to Thetis, with whom he lived for all those years. Yet he never became a sea-god and he never would. Eventually Thetis set him ashore, not far from where he had fallen, on the island of Lemnos in the north Aegean. He grew up there and continued his work as a blacksmith. One day, thinking over the events of his early life, Hephaistos began to make a throne. It was of solid gold and silver, encrusted with precious stones, studded with pearls. He worked on it with the help of his friends, the native gods of neighbouring Samothrake, the dwarfish Kabeiroi, who were artisans like himself.

'Take this to Olympos for me,' he said to them when it was finished. 'As you know, I am not welcome there. Give it to my mother Hera, and tell her it is a gift from me. It will demonstrate to her how little distress I now feel over her rejection of me.'

The Kabeiroi did as he said. Wisely, they did not wait to observe Hera's reaction to the unexpected gift; they were as modest and retiring as many other true craftsmen. Having delivered the gift and its accompanying message they departed in haste.

Hera admired the throne. She knew all about the progress of her rejected son, though she had never seen him since the day of his fall from Olympos. She was surprised and pleased that he had sent a fine specimen of his work as a personal gift to her. She sat on her new throne, sank back into it – it was very comfortable – and considered whether to send him a present in return. Somehow, if she did so, she must make it clear that he need not expect to be invited to Olympos. Having reached her decision, Hera tried to rise from the throne.

She was unable to move.

'Zeus!' she cried. 'Help me!'

Zeus was astonished by her urgent tone: his wife was seldom, if ever, helpless. He looked in from the next room. Hera was in a posture of perfect relaxation, yet her face expressed fear.

'I cannot move,' she said.

Zeus stepped forward, surprised that she did not even raise her arms as he approached. 'Are you ill?' he enquired.

'No, you fool. I'm trapped in this chair. Get me out of it.'

But Zeus, who can do anything he wishes, could not do this.

'Only a member of our own family could oppose my strength in this way,' said Zeus.

'It's my firstborn. It's Hephaistos who sent me this throne.'

'Then only Hephaistos can set you free,' said Zeus. His brother Poseidon and his sons Ares and Apollo all attempted to release Hera, but, of course, Zeus was right: it was impossible.

'We must ask Hephaistos to release her, then,' said Hermes. As the divine messenger he was familiar with the delicate negotiations that were often required to keep the peace on Mount Olympos.

The war god Ares, son of Zeus and Hera after their marriage, felt that Hephaistos and he ought to have a special sympathy for one another. After all, the swords and shields manufactured by Hephaistos were generally used by mortals in the service of Ares. He was wrong, as it turned out. He conscientiously paid a visit to his exiled brother and attempted to persuade him to release their mother from the throne, but Hephaistos dismissed him coldly.

'He wants to live among us,' Ares reported to the assembled immortals. 'I see now that he has never forgiven you, Mother, for throwing him down from Olympos.'

'He's misshapen,' said Hera coldly. 'A cripple. He wouldn't fit in. Anyway, he couldn't manage the stairs.'

'We must consider this seriously,' said Zeus. 'He is an immortal, and we cannot change the fact. Is it appropriate that he should remain apart from us, in permanent exile, through no fault of his? Now as a blacksmith, it appears to me, he will not find much to interest him here. Unlike mortals, who are always trying to kill one another, we have little use for the swords he makes. In any case, he cannot even make them here. Where are the volcanic fires that he needs to work his bronze and iron? They are under the Earth. Believe me, whatever we now decide,

Hephaistos will spend most of his time in the cavernous depths of Mount Etna, or in Stromboli, or the fume-filled caves of Lemnos and Samothrake. Meanwhile, if we enjoy using the gold cups and platters that he himself has made for us, why should we not invite him to enjoy them alongside us?'

'He'll smell of smoke,' Hera said, but her opposition was wavering.

'My suggestion,' said Hermes, 'is that we ask my half-brother Dionysos to speak to him on our behalf. He, too, is in exile on Earth.'

Hera was about to object. Dionysos, known to many as Bacchus, was Zeus's son by a beautiful mortal, Semele, and anger welled up in Hera's heart whenever she heard his name. But Hermes looked straight at her, and Hera merely said: 'I have to get out of this throne!'

Dionysos, as it turned out, was glad of the excuse to visit Lemnos. He had been wanting to thank Hephaistos personally for the beautiful coronet of rubies given by the Horai to his wife, Ariadne, as a wedding present, for it could not be doubted that the coronet was the work of Hephaistos. He took with him his constant companions the Satyrs, led by their father Seilenos and accompanied as usual by a wild band of women devotees, the Mainads.

Hephaistos knew nothing much of Dionysos, but he had heard of the grape and the wonderful liquor that Dionysos fermented from its juice. Such fancy products were of no interest to simple working people such as himself, he thought. However, since Dionysos had brought a full wineskin with him, Hephaistos felt that he could scarcely refuse to taste it. He was about to swig it directly out of the skin, but Dionysos politely dissuaded him.

'You need to enjoy the aroma as you are drinking,' he said. 'Those wide, shallow cups that you make yourself are ideal for the purpose.'

'I always thought people drank water from them.'

'It may have been so once,' said Dionysos with quiet pride. 'I believe I have been instrumental in changing the fashion. So, what do you think of it?'

'Give me some more,' Hephaistos answered. 'It's strong, isn't it?'

'Many people mix it with water.'

'Mere men, I imagine. Gods would know better. Even women know better, to judge by your Mainads over there.'

'How right you are,' said Dionysos.

By the time that Hephaistos had enjoyed his first tasting of wine to the full, he had become a good deal more mellow. He had forgotten that there was work to do in his blacksmith's shop. He had forgotten that he had recently refused Ares's request to release Hera on any terms. He had forgotten that he would never forgive his mother for throwing him out of Olympos. He had not quite forgotten that he fancied having a house on Mount Olympos himself.

'They need me there,' he confided to Dionysos. 'Right now, you know, my mother, Hera, is trapped in her new throne. She can't get out of it!'

'I was meaning to bring that up,' said Dionysos. 'If you were living up there on Mount Olympos, I suppose you could set her free?'

'Oh, easily,' Hephaistos reassured him. 'One of the first things I'd do.'

'And you might put in a word for me, afterwards,' said Dionysos wistfully. As the target of Hera's enmity he too, though a son of Zeus, was compelled to lead the life of a mortal, wandering the Earth.

But Hephaistos seemed to have fallen asleep.

Most people have seen paintings of the rowdy procession that ensued. It is a scene just as popular with artists of the Renaissance and after as with ancient Greek vase painters. Dionysos was in his golden chariot drawn by leopards; Seilenos was riding on his donkey; and Hephaistos, the only reason for the whole excursion, was sunk in hoggish slumber, snoring loudly, carried towards the mansions of the gods on the shoulders of many Satyrs. Other Satyrs and Mainads milled around them, singing, dancing and occasionally chasing one another into the bushes on either side of the road that led from Maroneia, on the coast of Thrace, westwards in the direction of the sacred mountain. Even for gods and drunken humans it was a journey of several days.

When they reached the gates of Olympos, Dionysos, who still hoped to be allowed in one day, and Seilenos and his crew, who had never been very interested, stood aside to line the route. Hephaistos, feeling much better by now, kissed a slow goodbye to several of the Mainads and limped proudly into the city which would from now on be his home. Zeus was there at the gate to welcome him.

'My dear fellow,' said Zeus, 'I am so happy you are to join us. Now, no need to look back. Here among us you will have everything you need.'

Hephaistos seemed suddenly to be in doubt, none the less. He was looking back through the gate, as it began to close, with an expression of regret.

'Nice girls,' he said.

Zeus recalled the recent arrival of Venus, and the immediate desire that seized every one of the gods of Olympos, married or single, to make her his wife. He himself had felt this dangerous urge as strongly as any of them. He had put it aside, of course; his life was complicated enough already. But what of Poseidon? Ares? Apollo? Even Hermes? If he were called upon to choose between them, how could he possibly arrive at a choice? And what eternal resentment must he face from those he did not choose?

He made a decision. The king of the gods makes decisions quickly, and never changes his mind. Why should he? He is always right. He decided that there would be no competition.

'You have no need to regret those mortal women,' he said. 'They are beautiful, but their beauty does not last. Come. There is someone I want you to meet.'

If it were conceivable that Zeus made a mistake on this occasion, his mistake would lie in not asking Venus for her opinion. If Zeus had thought to ask, he would also have found that even Hephaistos was far from enthusiastic. Like Venus, he was a newcomer to Mount Olympos. He had barely had a chance to meet the people with whom he would henceforth be living, but he had particularly noticed Athene as the introductions were made. What a demure, serious-minded young woman – and at the same time how perfect her features! How modest were her downcast grey eyes, and yet how they flashed with hidden fire! And, by all accounts, she was quite an intellectual. Hephaistos had often felt that he would like to share his life with someone of real intelligence. They would have plenty to talk about. He would speak to Zeus on the subject as soon as the chance arose, he promised himself …. But now, no sooner had he met Athene but he must forget her and accept this arranged marriage to Venus. She was a striking girl, no doubt about that, more lovely than any of the Mainads and probably just as passionate: but surely she was too young for him! Hephaistos had seen something of the world, and he knew quite well that an older man like himself, with simple, practical interests, not especially good-looking, walking with a pronounced limp, would face real difficulty in holding on to a beautiful young wife. He realized that he was already weighing up his potential rivals. Surely that was a bad omen for a marriage.

As for Venus, she was still thinking about the young gods she had seen at dinner. Hermes, so lively and amusing. Apollo, emotional but self-centred: he talked too much about himself, but how beautifully he sang! Poseidon, a rugged, mature, independent-minded person. And then there was Ares: very strong, perhaps dangerously strong if he became angry, but Venus felt that a relationship between a god and a goddess would be incomplete without the spice of danger. He had seemed to glance across at her rather often yesterday evening. His dark eyes had fixed on hers so that it had been difficult to look away … . So Zeus wanted her to marry this Hephaistos. Probably as a husband he would be kind and understanding; but that, she decided, could not be all there was to it. There must be passion. There must be danger.

There are many paintings of the entrance of Hephaistos to Olympos but there are few of the wedding of Hephaistos and Venus. No author describes the occasion. No author follows them to bed.

Their hearts weren't in it. As he lay with the most beautiful of all goddesses, more beautiful than any mortal, Hephaistos was still thinking of two particular Mainads, lively young women with an unconquerable enthusiasm for the sexual act and a comprehensive familiarity with its unofficial variations – skills that Venus, even though she was to be the goddess of love, had not yet developed (this was, after all, her first night). And although Hephaistos did his best to please her, and although she felt little pain as she lost her virginity, her thoughts even now returned repeatedly to Ares, his bold mind, resonant voice, dark eyes, tanned skin, muscular legs.

They had had a good talk, the day after their first meeting, even though neither of them had really very much to say. Ares, unlike Apollo, was diffident in company and assumed that she did not want to know all about his wars. Venus, two days after she rose from the sea, had as yet rather little experience of anything that could be distilled into small talk; and yet it seemed not to matter. They walked companionably, in the formal garden on which the dining room of Mount Olympos opened. Soon it happened that she stumbled on a stone in the path (though the gardens of Mount Olympos, like everything else about the halls of the gods, are perfect) and held on to his arm to steady herself. She continued to hold his arm, which was warm and strong. It had seemed that they were together only for a few minutes in all, yet when they turned to re-enter the palace the sun had moved far on his course.

And now she was married to Hephaistos; she had slept with Hephaistos. What would it have been like if she had gone to bed with Ares instead? And what would Ares say when they next met?

He said: 'I've been working on a small war in southern Greece: they're just about to start. It's beautiful countryside, and not far. Perhaps you'd like to see the place? We could be back by mid afternoon. Hephaistos won't miss you, will he?'

'No, that's all right,' said Venus. He's spending all day at his workshop on Lemnos. Let's go.'

They kissed, and it was good. They walked in the woodland at a shrine of Ares near the hill town of Tegea; they lay on the ground, and the pine needles made a kind of prickly bed for them; they tried the pleasures of sex, and those pleasures were very good. Mostly it was shadowy and cool in the wood, but sometimes the sun shone among the pine fronds straight into Venus's eyes, dazzling her for a moment; and then she looked back at Ares's face, above or beside her, and was happy. Venus was certain now, though she had been doubtful of it when lying in Hephaistos's bed, that she would enjoy being goddess of love.

That is how it often was for Ares and Venus: a couple of hours during the morning or afternoon, hours that passed with astonishing speed, as if the sun was hurrying on his course to deprive them of their stolen pleasure. Yet Hephaistos, the only real artisan among the gods, seemed not to be in the least suspicious about what his wife might be doing when he was at work. At dinner she and Ares hardly even dared to glance at one another. On holidays, when Hephaistos did not work, they pined.

Then, one morning after Hephaistos had gone out early as usual, Ares met Venus as she was setting off for the marketplace.

'I have something for you,' he said, and brought out a gold necklace encrusted with emeralds.

'It's beautiful!' said Venus. 'It's almost as ...'

'I know what you were about to say: almost as beautiful as those your husband makes. You're right. But in any case I didn't make it myself. It was made by a goldsmith among the Scythians, who are good at making things with gold, and it was offered to me in my temple at Tanais, at the mouth of the River Don. I like it so much that I will make sure the warrior who offered it will win all his battles. And the reason I like it is that I think it will look beautiful on you. I think so, but of course I don't know for certain. Will you try it on for me?'

Venus took the chain and lifted it as if to put it around her neck.

'Yes, it will look good,' said Ares, 'but even better when it sparkles on the soft, pale skin of your body when you are naked. Let's go somewhere where you can undress for me and I'll put it on for you. Then we'll see if I'm right.'

'But I don't want to take a lovely necklace like this into the woods,' said Venus.

'Then why don't we go to your bedroom?' Ares said quickly. 'I know we can do it safely today. Yesterday evening Hephaistos was chatting to me at dinner: he said there is a festival among the Sintians, those strange wild people of Lemnos. He'll be there all day listening to their country talk. He'll be enjoying himself. Why should he have all the fun?'

Secretly Venus felt that this was a little unfair to her husband. She seemed to get at least as much fun as he did. Still, he hadn't even told her about his Sintians and their festival, let alone invited her to take part in it alongside him. So she put aside the scruples that she had felt about leading Ares to the very bed that Hephaistos had made for her.

'You haven't ever seen my bedroom, have you?' she said, and tugged at his hand. 'Come on then. Let's do it now.'

What Venus and Ares did not know was that the sun god, Helios, had been watching them for a long time. He is not a voyeur; not exactly: but, since he is the sun, he cannot help seeing when people enjoy the pleasures of sex in broad daylight, especially if they do it in the open air. Even when they are deep in some forest and think that they have escaped his gaze they are often wrong: there will be flashes of sunlight that filter through the leaves. Suddenly a young woman in the sexual act, shameless, enveloped in pleasure and thinking for the moment of one man only, will be dazzled by a beam of light. She has to know that at that moment Helios, the sun, has seen her, and has seen her lover's face reflected in her eyes.

There has been a widespread belief that, for whatever reason, it is improper – even sacrilegious – to perform the sexual act in daylight, under the sky. Those who do it none the less, and accept the risk of being observed by the gleaming eye of Helios, are often the people who ought not to be having sex at all because they have taken a vow of chastity or are married to someone else.

Helios's all-seeing eye is not his only inconvenient feature: also he is not inclined to keep secrets. Sweeping the shadows aside, he shows whatever he sees to anyone who is interested. Now in this case, since Hephaistos and Helios were personal friends – sharing a long-standing interest in fire and its uses – he made quite sure that one afternoon Hephaistos was present at the right place and time to catch a glimpse of Ares and Venus frolicking in the dappled sunlight somewhere on the wooded slopes of Mount Olympos.

So this was how it came about that at dinner the previous evening Hephaistos had spoken in some detail about the long day that he expected to spend with the Sintians of Lemnos, and had made sure that Ares had heard everything. The blacksmith god was not usually very forthcoming about his daily timetable: he had found, as a matter of fact, that the other gods were not very interested in his doings, though their admiration for his workmanship was unfeigned. Ares, who ought to have reflected that this conversation was strangely out of character for Hephaistos, instead thought only of what advantage he could derive from his knowledge of his rival's plans for the next day.

Venus took off her earrings, her long robe, her sandals – there are many Greek and Roman statues and figurines of Aphrodite or Venus taking off her sandals. She reached behind her head to unclasp her jewelled circlet, allowing her long hair to swirl free about her shoulders. Then she took off the embroidered band that she wore next to her skin. Ares watched.

'Try it on now,' he said, and as he approached she turned her back on him so that he could place the new collar around her neck and fasten the clasp at the back. She felt his body touching hers. She turned round, put her own arms around his neck, and kissed him. She undid the clasps that held his tunic at his shoulders: it fell to his feet.

'Do I look good in it?' Venus asked, feeling the warm gold of each link of the collar and the cooler surface of the heavy medallion that hung below it as if to signpost the valley between her breasts.

She lay back on the wondrously soft bed that Hephaistos had made, and stretched out her arms again to draw Ares down on to her. As they made love the sun suddenly shone full on her face from the southeastern window of the bedroom, and Helios saw her, dewy with sweat, quite naked but for the golden collar. She was hardly aware of the shaft of sunlight, and quite unaware of the person whose hand reached in at the window at that same moment.

Ares suddenly felt a remarkable sensation, as if a thousand threads as light as gossamer, criss-crossing like a fishing net, had spread themselves across his skin at the same moment – his neck, his broad back, his long legs, all the way to the soles of his feet. He said:

'What's that? ... Venus, I can't move!'

'I don't need you to move,' said Venus, and then: 'There's something on my hands: I can't see what it is. I can't move them! And my legs too. My toes – it's around my toes, and my feet are fastened together. Help me!'

'I can't move,' said Ares again. By the absence of the delicate sensation of the threads he could quite easily tell where Venus's hands were placed on his shoulders and where her feet came together, across his buttocks.

'If anyone comes in they'll see me.'

'Me too,' said Ares.

At that moment they heard the door open. Neither was able to turn to see who was there. Perhaps there was no one? The door had been left wide open, and the murmurs of the main street of Mount Olympos became audible beyond. Then they heard the voice of Hephaistos, loud enough to be heard as far as the marketplace.

'Father Zeus! Gods of Olympos! Come this way. This will make you laugh!'

And the murmur of the street became focused and grouped, as the gods began to make their way into Hephaistos's house to see what he had to show them.

'... Laugh, or perhaps blush,' Hephaistos went on, his voice still rather louder than usual. 'You are about to see how Venus shames me with her lust for Ares ...'

There was a burst of laughter at the door. Apollo (Venus was sure it was Apollo) had been the first to arrive. If only she could move her legs!

'Come and have a look at this,' said Apollo to Hermes.

'... I'm just a hopalong, I know,' Hephaistos was saying. 'You can see why she would choose a man with two good legs ...'

'Just look at her, uncle,' Hermes said under his breath. 'What a woman!' His uncle Poseidon laughed too, deeply and unmistakably, like the beginning of an earthquake.

Next came the husky but feminine voice of Demeter from the back of the group: 'What is all this?'

'No, no,' said a bass voice, Poseidon again. 'You goddesses don't want to bother with this. It's just Ares and Venus, you know. I rather expected it, I must say. We'll sort all this out. Leave it to us.' He must have turned to Hephaistos at this point, because he went on: 'Damned clever, old boy. How have you trapped them like that?'

'Come closer, then,' said Hephaistos. He was evidently very angry, yet the dominant note in his voice was pride. 'Come and see how they betrayed themselves.'

'Ah, now I see,' said the voice of Hermes, much closer. Venus, still unable to move her head, realized that by directing her eyes downwards she could see her own legs, still brazenly wrapped around Ares. Not far beyond them she could see the faces of Apollo and Hermes, heads together, observing the scene attentively rather as if they were a couple of midwives.

'Yes, I see it too: you've caught them in a net,' said Apollo. 'But how did you make it?'

'Bronze filaments,' Hephaistos replied.

'It's wonderfully fine work,' said Poseidon.

'They would be invisible to a mortal eye.'

'And yet extremely strong. I only hope you never need to make one for me! Well, you've caught your fishes. Poor young Ares can't move at all. You've got him in a fine position. They were really enjoying themselves, weren't they?'

'They have had enough of their embrace now, I think,' said Hephaistos. 'They are hoping to get away quickly, I suspect. Oh, no. My net will hold them right here until Zeus, who gave her to me in marriage, pays me back every single gift that I paid as her dowry, whether gold or bronze or precious stones. She is a beautiful woman, but she has wandering eyes.'

'Ares is a fast mover,' Hermes muttered to Apollo, 'but old Hopalong's caught up with him. Taken in adultery! He'll have to pay to get out of this.'

'Tell me, Hermes, son of Zeus,' Apollo replied, 'how would you like to get into bed with golden Venus and end up trapped in a net like that?'

'Apollo, son of Zeus,' said his thieving half-brother, 'even if I knew I was going to be caught in a net three times as strong as this one, and all you gods were going to be there watching me, and all the goddesses as well, I would still get into bed with golden Venus.'

Apollo laughed out loud at this. But Poseidon was no longer laughing.

'Let him go now, old boy,' he said to Hephaistos. 'I guarantee you – and you have all these gods as witnesses to my promise – that Ares will pay whatever fine you impose.'

Hephaistos took some time to consider this. At last, hesitantly, he unfastened the net, and suddenly Ares and Venus were no longer held motionless. Ares pushed himself up off the bed. He reached for his tunic and left the room quickly, not looking at the other gods. Venus, blushing, sat up, happening to meet no one's eyes. She reached down to the floor for her embroidered band, which no male god would dare to touch. Then she found her circlet, caught up her hair in it and reached behind her head to fasten the clasp, paying not the least attention to the many eyes that were still fixed on her. Finally she reached out for the long robe that she had discarded, and fastened it at her shoulder with its single brooch. She left the room unhurriedly, her expression calm, her eyes level.

Ares made his way to Thrace, on the north shore of the Aegean, a warlike country, and consoled himself with the lively festivities conducted by his worshippers at Ainos, happy that they knew nothing of recent events on Mount Olympos. As for Venus, once out of the door she ran for her chariot. Her faithful sparrows carried her to her own shrine at Paphos, where she had first stepped ashore. There the three *Charites*, the Graces, daughters of Zeus, came to her. They bathed her and rubbed her with ambrosial olive oil, such as immortals always use, and dressed her in clean and shining clothes. She was more beautiful than ever.

This is how the poet of the *Odyssey* tells the story, but he does not vouch for it. He is too clever for that. Instead, he carefully puts the whole episode into the lips of Demodokos, the blind poet of the Phaiekes. The affair of Ares and Venus and the trap set by her husband, Hephaistos, are the theme of the song that Demodokos sings in the marketplace of Scherie. As he sings he plays on his lyre, and boys and girls dance to the music.

Demodokos – a mere shadow, a fictional poet – is the only early source for the marriage of Venus to Hephaistos and its consequences. Yet we take it all seriously, as we take everything in the *Iliad* and *Odyssey* seriously. So we next have to explain how it comes about that in myths and images Venus is hardly ever paired off with Hephaistos: she is nearly always placed side by side with Ares.

Reflecting on the day's adventure Venus was easily able to guess who had given her away. She remembered how the sun had shone into her face at the precise moment when Ares entered her body, when she had eyes for no one but him. Then she remembered how the sun had dazzled her for an instant when she first lay with her lover in a woodland glade near Tegea. Clearly it was the sun, Helios, who had betrayed her secret to Hephaistos.

Ares, she thought, had behaved well in the circumstances. Helios and Hephaistos had worked together to brand him publicly an adulterer. It would have been foolish of him to show anger or to make a quarrel in which he could have counted on no one's support. It would have been pointless to weep and dishonest to beg Hephaistos's forgiveness. Had he done so, Venus would have despised him. The laws of gods and men decreed that what they did was wrong: so from now on they must be aware of watching eyes.

Hephaistos had made himself look foolish. If he had confronted Ares as soon as he knew of their affair they might have worked things out. As a result of this public display, all the gods were officially aware that he was a cuckold. It was clear, too, that when laying his plans he had not even paused to think whether he wanted to divorce Venus (and get back the dowry he had paid) or make Ares pay the adulterer's fine; as a result, he had run a risk of achieving neither. She thought the less of him.

Then Venus turned her thoughts to the three gods who had now seen her naked. Apollo and Hermes had been rather boyish about it, she felt. 'Come and look at this,' Apollo had said, as if she and Ares were performers in some cheap show. And again: 'How would you like to get into bed with Venus?' Venus did not mind being admired, but with these words Apollo seemed to be having intercourse with her coldly, at arm's length, by proxy. Hermes's frank praise of her was somewhat coarse, though spoken in an undertone. But Hermes was not really so bad. Venus preferred to remember his last words, which made him sound almost defiant in his response to Apollo: 'I would still get into bed with Venus!' She wondered if that were bravado, or whether, given the opportunity, he would hold to his word.

Poseidon had behaved honourably. He had laughed, as anyone would. But then he had negotiated for Ares's release; what was more, he had achieved it. Although he could not interfere between husband and wife – it was up to Hephaistos to deal with Venus – the actual result of Poseidon's negotiation was to allow Venus to escape from her embarrassing position with the least possible delay. He had even guaranteed the fine. Venus decided that at the first opportunity she must thank Poseidon in person for his good sense.

The opportunity was not long in coming: she found him at home late in the afternoon on the following day. He led her to the cloisters on the east side of his house, where the sun shines in the morning, and he showed her the deep well in one corner of the formal garden. First he drew up a pail of water, and let her taste the chill of it on her tongue. Then he pulled on a second rope, and up came a jar of nectar. It, too, was icy cold: it had been waiting for just such a moment as this. The conversation, after he had poured them each a cup of the sparkling liquor, was not as embarrassing as she thought it might be.

'My brother has been a perfect fool,' said Poseidon, a thing that he fairly often said. 'A perfect fool to marry a lovely young goddess like you to poor Hephaistos. Now Hephaistos is really not a bad fellow ...'

'He's been kind to me,' said Venus.

'... and a genius with his hands,' Poseidon continued, taking a good mouthful of nectar, 'but it's not enough for you, is it, Venus? I know that quite well. As soon as I saw you I thought: when she marries, that girl is going to need a strong man, a man of real character.'

'Did you really?' said Venus. 'Because I've wondered what you were saying, that first evening at dinner. You were looking right at me and you said something to Apollo ...'

'I cannot tell a lie,' said Poseidon. He took another mouthful of nectar to give him courage, the first time he had ever needed to. 'I'll tell you exactly what I was saying. "It's a lovely dress, and I look forward to removing it."'

'Yes, I was sure it was something like that,' said Venus, who admired Poseidon's straightforwardness quite as much as his rugged looks. She rewarded him with a long kiss full on the lips.

Poseidon did not need to take off the dress, because the brooch at Venus's shoulder unfastens itself at the right moment. They lay down on the soft grass. The sun had passed behind the roof-ridge, and no one saw what they did.

Afterwards he said:

'I'll speak to my brother about it all when he's in a good mood. No, I don't mean for myself. I know perfectly well I'm too old for you. But we can't have you and Ares moping. I've never seen him look so pale as the morning of your wedding. I really believe he didn't eat a mouthful that day. Just imagine, the war god, off his food over a little ... over a goddess. Zeus will just have to let you two get together, and find another girl for Hephaistos. In fact I know just the one: she's one of the three

Graces. The one in the middle.'

'He'll like her,' said Venus immediately.

It really happened as Poseidon said it would. The poet of the *Iliad*, perhaps not familiar with the idea that there are three Graces, tells us simply that Hephaistos was married to Charis ('Grace'). Hesiod, in the *Theogony*, says that Hephaistos's wife was Aglaia, the youngest of the Graces. Neither of these authors seems to know that he ever married Venus.

No one mentions Venus's marriage to Ares, yet they give the impression of having been a married couple. On the timescale of Greek mythology they were together for a long time. In the dance of the gods and goddesses, in the Homeric *Hymn to Apollo*, Ares and Venus are side by side. At Sparta, said the traveller Pausanias, there was a temple of 'Aphrodite *Areia*' – 'Aphrodite of War', or 'Aphrodite of Ares' – with statues as ancient as any in Greece. Pausanias tells us also of the famous chest in which Kypselos, king of Corinth, was hidden by his mother when he was a child: by his descendants this chest was dedicated in the temple of Zeus at Olympia. Among the many vignettes carved on its wooden sides was one that depicted *Enyalios*, the war god otherwise called Ares, in full armour, leading Venus (as his captive? or his slave?). The poet of the *Iliad* makes Venus and Ares close friends, if not married then certainly a couple. When Venus is wounded by Diomedes on the battlefield of Troy, she begs her *dear brother* Ares to lend her his horses for a getaway. So when the gods begin fighting one another, on one traumatic day of the Trojan War, and the unlucky war god has been felled by a stone wielded by warlike Athene, his 'sister' Venus is naturally at hand to help him crawl away.

Those who make genealogies of the Greek and Roman gods can find three children that Venus bore to Ares – rather a large number for a casual affair. Her biographer must at least tell you the names of these children. The first two will grow up to be Ares's followers, Phobos and

Deimos ('Fear' and 'Terror'). They are his ideal companions, almost as close to him as his sister and best friend, Eris, whose name means 'Discord': fear and terror are the emotions that the war god takes into battle and they fight on his side. Even to modern readers, even to those who do not take mythology seriously, Phobos and Deimos are still familiar: they are the names of the two satellites of the red planet that hangs in the night sky like a drop of blood and is still named after Ares's Roman equivalent, Mars.

The third child of Venus and Ares is quite a different character. She was called Harmonia ('Harmony'); with a name like that she was certainly no companion of the war god. Harmonia is unusual among goddesses in that she married a mortal. Her husband was Kadmos, the Phoenician who brought knowledge of the alphabet to Greece, settled there and founded the city of Thebes. The Olympian gods attended the wedding of Kadmos and Harmonia and gave them rich gifts. There were children of that marriage: one of them was Semele, who was once the lover of Zeus, conceived his son Dionysos, and was killed by Zeus's thunderbolt.

One more way in which Venus and Ares resemble a married couple is that they were unfaithful to one another from time to time.

On one notorious occasion Venus discovered that Ares and Eos, the goddess of the dawn, were conducting an affair. Just as with the sun god Helios, any irregular behaviour by Eos is difficult not to notice: if she stays too late in bed, the world remains in darkness. And so, when the usually cloudless skies of Mount Olympos were strangely overcast one morning, Venus was puzzled. She looked round for Ares: perhaps he would know the explanation. But Ares, though not usually an early riser, was nowhere to be seen. She soon found the explanation for herself. Brightness, as at the dawning of a fresh spring morning, was visible around the closed door of one of the bedrooms of their palace. Venus looked inside, and found Eos, radiant and naked, engaged in vigorous sex with Ares.

Blushing pink, Eos returned to her proper place in the eastern sky. She learned that it is unwise to offend Venus, who has special powers of her own and took her revenge by decreeing that Eos should be for ever stung by sexual desire, like it or not, and that the targets of her insatiable desire should be mortal men. If this was a curse – immortals would undoubtedly have agreed that it was – Eos certainly suffered from it. At one period she felt unbearable desire for Kleitos, and snatched him away from his home on earth to live among the immortals. Kephalos was another of her targets; their son, said Hesiod, was Phaethon. Eos also desired Orion: he too was taken to live on Mount Olympos, but he was killed, it was said, either for challenging Artemis at quoits, or for attempting to rape Opis the Hyperborean, or (the worst crime of all) for assaulting Artemis herself. At any rate Artemis sent a scorpion to kill him; yet he survives as one of the most splendid constellations in northern skies. Apart from all these, Eos's most famous lover was Tithonos, whose tragic story is to be told in the words of Venus herself in chapter five.

3

The Children of Venus

IN AFTER YEARS POSEIDON AND VENUS, EQUAL IN THEIR INDEPENDENCE of mind, well-matched in their admiration for one another, met again from time to time. It is said that they had two children: a boy, Herophilos, and a girl called Rhodos. Her name means 'rose', a beautiful name, but Rhodos is also the name of the island of Rhodes of which she was the patroness. Her beauty eventually attracted the unblinking eye of the sun god Helios. He and Rhodos were lovers, it was often said, and the people of Rhodes built a colossal statue of Helios to guard their city and its harbour.

Venus could never be bound to anyone by marriage. She personifies sexual desire, which is by its nature unrestricted. She desired Ares and slept with him. She desired Poseidon and slept with him. In any case, why need she accept any such rules? She knew that her first husband, Hephaistos, had attempted unfaithfulness, even if he had not quite achieved it: he had made a pass at Athene (of all people), probably on a day when Venus had been particularly cold to him. Athene, as it happened, came to his forge that day to ask him to make a breastplate for her. With the flimsy excuse of measuring her for a good fit, Hephaistos reached out to embrace her. The virginal Athene backed away hastily, but he was not so easily discouraged: they struggled, and Hephaistos, clumsily attempting to rape her, spilt his sperm on her leg. In disgust Athene wiped it off with a skein of wool and threw it on the earth. The child Erichthonios was born from this skein of wool, and he is counted as the son of Hephaistos and Gaia 'Earth'. Venus already knew of this unedifying scene. What was more, her favoured lover, Ares, had set her the example: he had shown utter disregard for the laws of marriage during their early affair.

Remembering the words that Hermes had spoken as she lay trapped by her husband's cruel net, Venus decided to find out whether Hermes really meant it.

'In my bedroom,' she said to him, 'when Hephaistos called you all in as witnesses, what was it exactly that you and Apollo were saying?'

'I hardly remember ...' Hermes began.

'Oh, yes, you do. Didn't Apollo ask you whether you would like to be in Ares's place? And what did you reply?'

At this point Hermes, like Poseidon before him, felt the need for a mouthful of nectar.

'I said yes. I'm sure you heard me. I said I would get into your bed even if I knew it was a trap.'

'So what are you going to do about it?' Venus demanded. 'I won't wait for ever.'

Which explains how young Hermes, Zeus's favourite son, the messenger of the gods, found himself climbing into bed with Venus later that day. She had not realized (because he is very modest about it) that Hermes was a symbol of male sexuality all over Greece: you could not go far along any street before you saw a simple stone pillar which would be topped by Hermes's bearded head and punctuated, about half way up, by an erect phallus. At any rate, Venus was not disappointed. The child that she bore nine months later was, however, rather unusual. Unusual indeed would be the offspring of a symbol of male sexuality and a symbol of women's sexual power. Their child shared both their names – being called Hermaphroditos – and both their natures, having both male and female sexual parts. Hermaphroditos is a god, but from time to time is born and reborn among mortals, and through sharing in the different physical natures of mortal men and women is easily recognized as something greater and more portentous than either – as a divinity, in fact.

That is how the Greek historian Diodoros of Sicily understood the story. The Roman poet Ovid, in *Metamorphoses*, tells it very differently. Hermaphroditos, child of Venus and Mercury, resembled both his parents (as children naturally do) but was born male, and was brought up by the Naiad nymphs of Mount Ida, not far from the ancient city of Troy. Eventually, as a handsome adolescent, Hermaphroditos began to travel the world. Walking purposefully southwards he reached the region then called Caria (the island of Rhodes lies close offshore). There he came to a mountain spring that fed a clear woodland pool and belonged to a solitary nymph, the only one who never joined in with the rest and never took part in the hunting expeditions led by Artemis. Instead she spent her time beautifying herself and admiring the result; the clear water of her pool served her as a mirror. The name of the nymph, and of the spring too, was Salmakis.

Salmakis desired Hermaphroditos from the first moment she saw him. Making herself look as beautiful as she knew how, she emerged from the surrounding woods and begged him to be her husband, or – if he was already married – her lover. But Hermaphroditos knew nothing as yet of the pleasures shared by men and women. He blushed, hesitated, refused, and as she pressed her argument he began to panic and to look for an escape.

'Please forget it,' said Salmakis, retreating. 'I leave you in peace, then, to the enjoyment of this spring.'

No longer inhibited by her presence, he realized how much he wanted to bathe in the cool waters of the pool, and he stripped and began to swim. Salmakis was watching him from the bushes, and when she saw his handsome naked body she ran out at once. Throwing off her clothes she dived into the pool and gripped him in a passionate embrace in the water, as if to force him to the sexual act whether he wished it or not. But Hermaphroditos still resisted. Salmakis cried out to the gods with this prayer: 'Unite him to me! Join us so that we shall never more be parted!' Did she foresee the result? The gods heard her prayer and joined their two bodies into one, a body that was now both male and female, hermaphrodite.

No one in later times has dared to swim in the spring of Salmakis – except those few who have done so intentionally, in full knowledge of the consequences, and have emerged from the water with a new sexual identity.

Even the latest newcomer to Mount Olympos, the wine god Dionysos, was privileged to take his turn in Venus's bed. It was a less rewarding experience for her than some others. Dionysos was never able to relax fully, even in bed, even after his apotheosis. Hera hated him, not so much for himself as for his origin: he was the child of Zeus and of a mortal girl, Semele, and at the time of that affair Zeus had promised to divorce Hera and make Semele queen of the gods in her place. He had not been able to keep his promise: Hera had seen to that, but she continued to resent Dionysos. Perhaps, then, she cursed the bed that he and Venus shared; or else she cursed Venus's subsequent pregnancy. Venus lay in at her shrine at Lampsakos, on the Hellespont, and when baby Priapos was born she knew at once that she could not possibly take him to Mount Olympos with her. His facial features seemed normal enough (though, to tell the truth, he eventually had a somewhat feminine look, just like his father Dionysos) but Priapos was abnormal in one very specific way. Sexually he was quite excessively well endowed.

At Lampsakos, his home city, Priapos eventually had a famous temple and was worshipped with regular festivals attended not only by citizens but by many strangers. All across the Mediterranean there were statues of Priapos, armed with a sickle and an erect, red-painted phallus, strategically placed at the entrance to orchards and vineyards to warn intruders of the painful punishment that awaited them for theft. To those who did not steal fruit, Priapos was a familiar and friendly god. Men and women alike would pray to him for good sex and fertility; they wreathed his statues in gratitude for favours bestowed. Men who were troubled by impotence would know that they had somehow offended Priapos, and make offerings in his temples to appease his anger.

He was not dignified enough for Mount Olympos.

Some, including the poetess Sappho, credit Venus with another child, a daughter, *Peitho* whose name means 'Persuasion'. In his poem addressed to the prostitutes of Venus's temple at Corinth to be quoted in chapter seven, Pindar calls these slaves of the love goddess *handmaids of Persuasion.* She is in truth an abstraction, one of the many qualities that surround the idea of sexual desire. So are two occasional attendants of Venus, *Zelos* ('Jealousy') and *Apate* ('Deceit'). Like Priapos in one way, and like Eros in another way, Persuasion, Jealousy and Deceit are qualities that contribute to making the works of Venus a reality.

Thus, having dealt with Hermaphroditos and Priapos and Peitho, we now need to trace the origin of Eros.

We think of him as Venus's best-known child, but on this matter opinions among Greek authors differed. Some saw him as having come into existence without any parentage, the fourth and last of the ancient divine forces that made the world. Others, more poetically minded, made him the son of Zephyros, the west wind, and Iris, the rainbow; or else of Nyx, night, and Erebos, the lower darkness; or else of Gaia, the earth, and Ouranos, the sky, who were the parents of Dione also. According to some he was one of the Harpyes, the avenging demons who punish humans for their worst misdeeds: by true pessimists love may certainly be viewed in this way. But all these and others are minority opinions. The majority felt that he was the son of Venus, which is logical enough, since sexual desire may be seen as the origin of love; but who was his father? It was Ouranos, thought Sappho; it was Ares, Venus's lifelong companion, thought Simonides; it was Hermes, so others believed. It was Zeus, some said, but others denied that Zeus ever slept with Venus.

Venus, whom we call the love goddess, presides over the harmonious pleasures that male and female enjoy together. Whenever Eros came into being as a god, love in its fullest sense – the love of one human for another, the love that includes sexual desire and so much else as well, the love that is like the piercing of an arrow and the flick of a whip – came into being at the same moment. It cannot well have existed before that time.

Eros, whose weapons tear the skin and pierce the heart, makes love exclusive, and makes it hurt. He is the 'loosener of limbs'; he makes people shake, or quake, with uncontrolled passion; he forces them together with his famous arrows; he captures them and ropes them together; in classical Greek vase paintings he will be seen driving a woman into her lover's arms with a blazing torch or with a whip. Love is painful; Eros causes this pain.

As to his parentage, in any case, we had better accept the majority opinion. Sexual desire is the natural antecedent of love; therefore Venus gave birth to Eros. This at least explains the many pictures in which Venus is a beautiful young woman and Eros is a mischievous child. She was the mother who taught him all she knew and was sometimes displeased by the use he made of his skills, especially if he turned his weapons upon her – witness the paintings that show a crying Eros from whom Venus has temporarily confiscated his bow and arrow.

On the other hand, as soon as she knew Eros's nature and powers, Venus knew that she needed him. Not so much for the animals (over whose sexual pleasures she presides equably) but for humans and gods, who sometimes think they are too clever for sex. Eros, she knew, would keep them in line.

Contradicting the evidence of those pictures, therefore, Venus often encourages Eros in his mischief-making. For example, she had found it hard to forgive Helios for betraying the secret of her affair with Ares. With her naughty son's help she now punished Helios for this betrayal. They arranged it between them that Helios would have a love affair, and that everyone would know about it, and that he, too, would be betrayed.

Helios glows with solar fire every day, but thanks to an arrow from Eros's quiver he now began to burn with a different kind of fire. Instead of shining down unblinkingly on all the world, his eye became focused on a single mortal girl, Leukothoe, daughter of Orchamos who in those far-off times was king of the fortunate and aromatic land of Arabia. According to the writers of Greek myth, this Orchamos was seventh in line of direct descent from Belos or *Baal*, king of the gods of Phoenicia. Orchamos had married Eurynome, the most beautiful woman in all the East, and Leukothoe was their child.

Everyone knew that Helios had fallen in love because love

compelled him to change his daily routine. He would rise quickly in the morning to catch an early glimpse of Leukothoe, and go to bed late at night because he could not tear himself away from the sight of her, and so the winter days were longer than they had ever been; yet at the same time the sun's light was fainter and sometimes shadowed, ringed with darkness. He was sick with love.

One evening he felt that he could no longer bear the pain of separation from Leukothoe. Leaving his horses to browse in their pastures at the western end of the world, he crept along its southern edge, behind the mountains of the moon, and thus, almost unnoticed, he reached Arabia. He stood before Leukothoe, where she sat quietly spinning wool, and pleaded with her to accept him as her lover. When she understood who he was – he shone so brightly that she could scarcely bear to look at him – she dared not refuse him, and took him to her bed. But Helios already had a lover, the nymph Klytie. At Venus's urging Eros sent off another arrow. Its poisonous effect was to fill Klytie with jealous love for Helios. She could not endure the thought that he had given his love to someone else, and she complained to Orchamos that his daughter had given away her virginity. In vain Leukothoe pleaded with her father that she could not have resisted the power of the sun. In accordance with the strict laws of the Arabs he and his people stoned her, so that the heap of stones became her grave. Even Helios himself, however brightly he shone on these stones next day, could not restore the warmth of life to her battered body.

There is only one recorded occasion on which the love goddess and her mischievous son disagreed seriously. It is a story told in Rome: it was apparently known in Greece, but there is scarcely any literary evidence of the fact. In this story, therefore, the young god is not named Eros, as elsewhere in the book, but Cupid, from his Latin name *Cupido* ('Desire, Lust'). My retelling is based on the incomparable narrative of Apuleius.

There was once a young princess in a certain city, and her name was

Psyche. She was so astonishingly beautiful that all the citizens began to think of her as Venus in person. They and the people of the neighbouring cities ceased to attend the temples of Venus and no longer made offerings at her altars. The wreaths that had been placed around votive inscriptions in praise of the works of Venus dried out and grew dusty and were not replaced. The festivals of Venus no longer attracted crowds: instead these crowds came to see the princess Psyche whenever she appeared in public and to follow her in procession wherever she went. Psyche was almost too young and innocent to understand that she was depriving a powerful goddess of the worship that was her due; Psyche's father, the ruler of the city, was too complacent to trouble himself over the matter. He felt sure that his daughter would make a magnificent marriage, having attracted such widespread attention, and he consulted the oracle of Apollo at Didyma on the matter. This is what the oracle told him:

> King, place your girl on the pinnacle of the highest mountain
> Adorned with the panoply of a deathly wedding.
> Know this. Your future son-in-law is not of mortal kind:
> Savage, untamed, poisonous like a viper
> He wings his way across the aether, wearying
> And exhausting all creatures with his weapons and his fire.
> Jove himself trembles at him and the gods are afraid
> And rivers turn to ice and the lower darkness shivers with fear.

Horrified by this ruling, Psyche's father and mother nevertheless obeyed the god's instruction. The procession that led Psyche to the mountain top bore greater resemblance to a funeral than a wedding. The guests wore black garments and carried spluttering torches. Flute players performed the most mournful of melodies; cries of anguish were heard on all sides. Psyche herself led the way bravely, though she could not guess what lay in store.

Left alone on the mountain as the celebrants retreated, Psyche found herself lifted by a gentle breeze and carried to an unknown valley, lush with gardens and orchards. She was set down at the steps of a magnificent palace, whose doors opened silently to admit her. She wandered through its rooms and cloisters and realized that music was playing as if to greet her, though she could see no musicians. Feeling hungry, she found that she was passing a dining couch and table, laden with delicacies. Dishes and cups found their way to her hands, yet she saw no one serving her. And then at last the sky darkened and she felt that it was time to sleep. Unseen gentle hands led her to her bedroom and helped her to prepare for her wedding night. Then they left her. But when it was quite dark she felt a movement on the bed and knew that her husband was there. He took her tenderly in his arms and made love to her, and she was not at all frightened. They slept together, but very early in the morning, before there was any light, she was sleepily aware that he was leaving her. She went to sleep again, and when it became light the invisible maids were round her again, reassuring her that all was well and that her husband would return next evening.

And so he did. Now, for the first time, Psyche spoke to him. 'I want to love you,' she said, 'but first I must see you. I want to know who you are. Won't you tell me?'

'Psyche,' he said, 'you are in mortal danger, and the danger will be even greater if the secret of my identity is revealed. Ask me no questions yet.'

Then they made love again; and so they did every night, and soon Psyche was pregnant with their first child.

It was a beautiful palace. Psyche was very happy there except that she was all alone. She was already almost in love with her husband, but since she was now going to have his baby she wanted all the more to know who he was and what he looked like. So she waited for a time when none of the invisible maids seemed to be near, and went and looked into the palace kitchens and found an oil lamp used by the baker, who fortunately always began his work before it was light. She hid this lamp behind a curtain in her bedroom. That night, after she and her husband had made love and he was sleeping peacefully, she picked up the lamp and lit it.

Of course she knew at once who he was. He was a beautiful young man with two strong, feathery wings at his shoulders (strange that she had never felt them) and there, discarded on the floor, were his bow and quiver (strange that she had never heard the arrows rattle). Just to make sure, she took out one of those arrows and tested its point. She pressed too hard: it pricked her finger, and so when she glanced back at the figure in her bed she was at once hopelessly in love with him. She had been pricked by one of Love's arrows, and she was in love with Love himself – with the god Cupid. She trembled with the force of her desire. As she trembled, the hot oil in the lamp spilt over, and a few drops landed on his shoulder. In a moment he was awake.

'Psyche,' he said, 'you have lost me now. Yes, I am Cupid. You allowed yourself to be worshipped in place of my mother Venus, and she told me to use my arrows to punish you for your sacrilege. She wanted me to make you fall in love with some despised and wicked man. But when I saw you for myself, I fell in love with you! I was foolish enough to think that I could marry you secretly and that my identity would not be revealed. There is no hope of that now. We must part, and I must try to make my peace with her.' And with that, although Psyche tried to hold him back, he opened his wings and flew off to Mount Olympos.

Cupid's fears were justified. Perhaps it was not Psyche herself who gave away the secret. Perhaps it was the invisible servants of his palace who talked to other servants in other divine palaces. Perhaps it was the Olympian gods themselves who had observed both the disappearance of Psyche and the continual absences of Cupid. At any rate, Venus now knew all about her son's love for Psyche and she was angry.

'This girl, a mere mortal, fit only to be my slave, dared to set herself up as my rival! I told you to make her fall in love with some despicable mortal, not to sleep with her yourself! Do you take me for a procuress, you shameless boy? No, you are not married to her. That, at any rate, is certain. Slaves cannot marry.'

And she locked him in his room, telling the other gods merely that the burn on his shoulder needed time to heal. They knew perfectly well that poor Cupid was in trouble again. Psyche, meanwhile, filled with sadness, had left the wonderful palace where she had spent the happiest months of her life. As she set out across the valley the buildings crumbled into dust behind her.

Not knowing which way she was going, and having no idea where she might find sanctuary, she wandered until she came to a temple of Ceres, whom the Greeks call Demeter, the goddess of vegetation and of the annual renewal of fertility.

'Help me!' she cried to the goddess, but Ceres, who knew her immediately, answered:

'Psyche, you are suffering under the anger of Venus. I cannot oppose her will. If you are hungry, eat this cake that was dedicated on my altar, and then go on your way. You must ask some other god for help.'

Psyche walked on further, hungry and footsore. Next she came to a shrine of Juno, whom the Greeks call Hera, the queen of the gods, who presides over marriage and childbirth.

'Help me, Juno!' she cried, but Juno said:

'Psyche, I have sympathy for all women who are faithful to their husbands, and for all who are carrying children, but I cannot help you. Venus claims you as her slave, and by the law of Rome a runaway slave girl may not claim sanctuary here. Drink your fill of water from the spring in my sanctuary, and then go on your way. You must go to Venus's own temple and beg her for mercy. I do not know if she will grant it.'

So Psyche walked on again, and eventually, nearly exhausted, she came to a temple of Venus not far from the walls of her own home city. As she approached it an old woman, a former prostitute, one of the other slaves of Venus, saw her and knew who she was.

'You are Psyche!' she cried. 'You used to be our princess! Well, you are not a princess now; you are a runaway, our lady Venus tells us. This is my lucky day.'

Before Psyche could react the old woman had grabbed her by her long hair and was dragging her into the temple. She forced the girl to her knees before the altar, and cried triumphantly:

'Reward me, Venus! I have captured your runaway slave!'

'So, you little whore,' said Venus, 'we meet at last. Not only have you allowed the people of your city to acclaim you as the new Venus: you have gone on to seduce my poor son Cupid, who was too innocent to know how to resist you. And now you have burned him with hot oil. Tell me, if you owned a slave who behaved in such a way, what would you do with her?'

Psyche could only hang her head and say nothing. Yes, she was Venus's slave, a slave to love; she had never seen it in this way until now, but evidently it was true. Her mistress's second accusation was unjust, because she had not knowingly seduced Cupid and had not even known her secret lover's identity; but how could she explain this without throwing all the blame on him? He was probably in enough trouble already. In any case, the first and third accusations were just. Firstly, she had committed sacrilege against Venus; lastly, by disobeying her lover, she had burned his shoulder. She had earned the anger of Venus.

'Sorrow! Grief! Where are you, my faithful attendants? Take this disobedient slave and punish her,' said Venus.

Sollicitudo and *Tristities*, 'Sorrow' and 'Grief', who are indeed among the servants of the love goddess though not the ones most often celebrated, led Psyche away and whipped her mercilessly. Meanwhile Venus went to her son's room. The burn on his shoulder was healing only slowly, and he seemed meanwhile to be suffering from some less definable sickness. He ate hardly any ambrosia, and drank very little nectar. He appeared feverish, and never smiled. Venus had until now been concealing from herself what must be the cause of Cupid's sickness, but having seen the beauty of Psyche – even in her exhausted state – she could ignore the truth no longer. Her unfortunate son had been infected somehow by the poison from one of his own arrows, a poison for which there is no cure. He was in love.

Sorrow and Grief dragged Psyche into Venus's presence next morning; her only garment was stained grey with the dust of the cell where she had spent the night and red with blood from her whipping. They threw her to the ground before her mistress. Venus rose from her throne and descended the few steps to the cold floor on which Psyche was crouching. She reached out, grabbed a handful of Psyche's beautiful hair and tugged at it, pulling out many strands. She took hold of Psyche's shift and ripped it till it was little more than tattered strips of linen.

'Kneel, slave,' said Venus.

Psyche knelt before Venus, her eyes downcast, and did not speak.

'I have decided to allow my son to sleep with you,' said Venus, 'though why he should want to I cannot imagine. Henceforth you will be his slave; you will go to his bed as often as he sends for you. You are pregnant, I notice. Well, I may even allow the child to live – as a slave, of course. Like mother, like child. Notice my generosity. But first you will perform a simple errand for me. I wish you to take this box to Proserpina in the Underworld. Ask her for a little of her youthful beauty, because, thanks entirely to your wilful misbehaviour and clumsiness, I am looking rather careworn after attending my poor son's sick bed. I need to look fresh and young this evening at the Theatre of the Gods. Off you go now or you will not be back in time.'

Psyche was sure at once, whatever Venus might say about serving Cupid on her return, that this simple errand was a death sentence. Even immortals fear the journey to the Underworld, and few of them have dared to undertake it; it is true that one or two of those who have done so have been lucky enough to return. Psyche, however, was not an immortal.

She decided not to prolong the agony. She found a tall tower, not far from Venus's temple, and began to climb the stairs inside, intending to throw herself down from the top. That would surely be the quickest way to the Underworld, and thus she would at least fulfil the first half of Venus's instruction. Why make plans for a return journey? Mortals cannot return to life.

As she neared the top of the stairs an unearthly wail, coming from the darkness close beside her, startled her so that she almost fell. But Psyche had had many surprises in the last few days and was not to be frightened by this one. It was only an owl.

'Stop, Psyche,' said the owl. 'You are planning to kill yourself. You must not do it.'

'Venus wants me to go to the Underworld,' said Psyche. 'I'm sure she wants me to die, and I'm sure I will. So it's all the same.'

'She does indeed,' said the owl, 'but I am Athene, goddess of wisdom, and I know that you can carry out her orders and still return alive. I know, too, that my silly nephew Cupid still loves you as much as ever. For his sake, as well as yours, I will take you to the wild and windy Cape Taenarum, south of Sparta, where there is a cave that leads directly to the Underworld.

'Now if you are really to be the first mortal to visit the Underworld and return alive,' the owl continued, 'you must prepare yourself very carefully. Charon, the boatman on the river Styx, will ferry you across only if you are holding in your lips a silver obol: that is the standard fare. Take none, and you will not be able to cross the river at all; you will wander for endless years on this side of it. Take just one, and you will remain in the Underworld for ever. So I will give you two silver obols – good Athenian obols that carry my own image as Athene on one side and an owl on the other – and I warn you that you must keep the second obol well hidden until it is time for your return. There are many in the Underworld who would be glad to steal it from you if they knew of it. You will face another danger, the dog Cerberus. He will know that you are a living girl, and the living do not belong in the Underworld. His hair will bristle and he will unfailingly oppose your entrance. Nor does he allow any, living or dead, to return to the ferry. For Cerberus, too, you must take two gifts. Carry in each hand a good big piece of polenta. Throw the first to him as you enter, and be sure to keep the second safe until you are ready to leave. He gets plenty of carrion, but he especially likes polenta and it will keep his jaws busy.

'Proserpina will offer you a sumptuous meal while she fills Venus's box. Do not touch it. The Underworld is full of gastronomes, but if you eat any of the fine foods of that fearful place you must continue to eat them always, and therefore you will be unable to return. Do not blame Proserpina for this trick: she is very lonely, poor girl, during the six months of each year that she passes in the Underworld, in exile from Mount Olympos, and she would love to have a companion. Ignore all that she offers and ask her only for a crust of bread, which you may safely eat. Ignore all distractions on your journey. One more thing. However strong the temptation, do not look in the box. Give it to Venus untouched.'

So, with Athene's help, Psyche set out for the Underworld, laden with Venus's box, two big sticky lumps of polenta and two Athenian obols. Like others who visit the kingdom of the dead she was troubled with horrifying visions, people or wraiths who threatened to attack her, limbless beggars who demanded food from her. She herself would have been too soft-hearted to pass them by, and would never have reached her journey's end, but she obeyed Athene's instruction. Charon snatched an obol from her lips and was so distracted by her beauty that he took the oars himself to row her across the River Styx, an almost unheard-of event. Cerberus bayed menacingly, but was calmed by her sweet voice and deeply interested by the sticky polenta. After some hours of walking in the blackness of the Underworld, Psyche reached the palace and delivered her message to Proserpina – Persephone, the Maiden, as the Greeks prefer to call her.

'Why is poor Venus in need of beauty?' she asked.

'She has been up night and day, looking after Cupid, who has a burn on his shoulder from some spilt oil. And it's my fault: I spilt it.'

'You must be Psyche,' said Proserpina. 'I've heard a lot about you. Now sit down and have a nice meal before you set out on your return journey. We have some marvellous *foie gras*, just in today, and thanks to *pourriture noble* this year's sweet wines are the best ever. And while we're eating you can tell me what young Cupid is like as a lover.'

'I really can't manage anything,' said Psyche politely. 'Just a bit of bread, perhaps.'

Proserpina was disappointed but not surprised. 'Well, well, I'll look forward to seeing you on Mount Olympos when I return in the spring. We'll be friends then.'

'I don't go there. I'm only a mortal.'

'Wait and see,' said Proserpina mysteriously. 'I gather Cupid is still very much in love with you.'

Psyche made her return journey uneventfully, as far as the cave at Taenarum. Cerberus fawned, licked her feet, took the second lump of polenta gently from her hand, and went away quietly to eat it, leaving the gates of the Underworld temporarily unguarded. Charon was surprised to see her, but accepted the second obol without question and rowed her back across the River Styx.

It was already early evening. There was still time for Psyche to find a temple of Venus and complete her commission; but she was very tired. She sat down for a moment on the windy promontory of Taenarum, watching the white waves of the Aegean beat on the rocks far below, and wondered about the beauty that was in the box. She must deliver it to Venus, of course, but might she not have just a little of it for herself? Stiff and bruised from her whipping, tired and footsore after many hours of walking, Psyche, like Venus, felt more than usually in need of beauty. She opened the box; but it was empty after all. What had been the use of her errand?

Quite invisible to Psyche, the ingredients of beauty had been carefully packed in Venus's box. The lightest of these ingredients had naturally risen to the surface: it was peaceful Sleep. As soon as the box was opened, it escaped and spread gently over Psyche. She fell asleep at once.

Meanwhile Cupid felt so much recovered that afternoon that he decided to go for a walk in the gardens of Mount Olympos. Finding that his mother had locked him in his bedroom again, he flew straight out of the window. Fortunately he met his aunt Athene, who was able to tell him exactly where Psyche had gone and why. It will remain unknown whether Cupid would have dared to enter the cave at Taenarum and go down to the Underworld in search of her, but, as it turned out, he did not need to. As he hovered over the promontory in the gathering dusk, he spotted her, asleep on the grass.

He landed softly beside her, gently brushed the Sleep from her face and tipped it back into the box. Psyche woke, looked at the stars in the evening sky, and began to cry.

'I have been so foolish! Now there's no time left to take this box to Venus. She will punish me again, and I deserve it.'

'You deserve no such thing,' said Cupid, 'and I am very angry with my mother for treating you as her slave. Don't worry about the box: I will deliver it to her, and I can be on Mount Olympus in a moment. Now go back to the cave mouth. As you saw, it is a shrine to my great-uncle Neptune. He will be kind to you. You and I will meet again tomorrow.'

Cupid delivered the box, but he avoided seeing his mother. He left it with the Horai, who were due to attend her as she dressed for the theatre later that evening. Then he flew on to the palace of Jupiter, king of the gods, known to the Greeks as Zeus, and knelt at the foot of the throne.

'Dear grandfather,' said Cupid obsequiously, 'I need your help. I'm in love! Can you imagine how that feels?'

'Thanks to you, you mischievous fellow, I know very well how it feels. How many of your arrows have you used on me? At least half a dozen already. How dare you ask for my help?'

'There is a very beautiful mortal girl named Psyche. I cannot live without this girl, but my mother hates her. If I'm not allowed to marry her I will never use my arrows again.'

'Well, I will make her immortal for you, if that will help,' said Jupiter. 'But while we're on the subject, young man, it's a long time since I last had a holiday on Earth. Have you noticed any other very beautiful girls there just now?'

Meanwhile Neptune, whom the Greeks call Poseidon, had become aware that a mortal girl had sought sanctuary at his temple at Taenarum, and they were having a long talk.

'Cupid's mother and I have a close relationship,' said Neptune finally. 'I will speak to her tomorrow morning. I think I can persuade her to look more kindly on you. But tell me, my dear, have you any sisters? Any perhaps who are interested in the sea?'

And so it was arranged. Neptune arrived at Venus's palace in time for breakfast, which she always took in her bedroom. Taking full advantage of the situation, Neptune was easily able to persuade her that Psyche had done nothing that could not be forgiven. He pretended to blame himself for setting a bad example to Cupid and thus persuaded Venus that boys will be boys. He was so successful in his mission that when Jupiter came round later in the morning, he found that he need do nothing else but agree that it was time Cupid was married. His offer to make Psyche immortal was accepted with impatience.

'Of course she must be immortal,' said Venus. 'I would have thought that was obvious.'

Mercury, the messenger of the Roman gods, was sent to conduct Psyche from Cape Taenarum to Mount Olympus. The marriage took place that same day. Vulcan, whom the Greeks call Hephaistos, was the cook; the Horae decorated the whole palace with red roses and other suitable flowers; the Graces scattered droplets of a heavenly perfume, redolent of the balsam of Mecca; the Muses performed the wedding song. Apollo then sang to his own accompaniment on the lyre, and the music was so enticing that Venus and the Graces were the first to step forward to dance. Thus Psyche was married to Cupid, and none too soon. Their daughter, who was born soon afterwards, is called *Voluptas*, 'Pleasure'.

If any reminder is needed of the deadly pain that love (Cupid, Venus) can cause, it is supplied by carved gemstones that summarize the story of Cupid and Psyche. They show Psyche bound and captive, Cupid himself burning her with his torch.

4

The Story of Adonis

Venus's most famous lover is certainly Adonis. Now Adonis existed long before the Greeks gave him this name. To the peoples of ancient Mesopotamia he was already familiar: they called him Tammuz and Dumuzi.

As the Sumerians told the story, their love goddess, Inanna, decided to marry. She and her elder brother, Utu, the sun god, agreed on this, though at first they disagreed on the choice of husband. '*Who will share my bed with me, brother?*' she asked.

'Sister,' said Utu, 'let the shepherd Dumuzi marry you. His milk is good; his butter is good.'

'The farmer Enkimdu shall marry me,' said Inanna petulantly, 'the one who makes the wheat and flax grow.'

But the shepherd god Dumuzi spoke for himself:

'Whatever the farmer has, that man of ditches and dykes and ploughs, I have twice as much.' He strode across the meadow to fight Enkimdu, but he replied:

'Why should I fight the shepherd? His sheep may graze in my orchard; his lambs may drink from my ditches, and I will attend his wedding with Inanna!'

Now Inanna, the young wife of Dumuzi and the queen of Heaven and Earth, once dared to lay claim to a third realm, the Underworld, where her sister, Ereshkigal, was queen. On her head she placed the crown of the land between the rivers. She wore her necklace of lapis lazuli beads around her neck, her band of pearls *en sautoir* crossing between her breasts, and her royal robe. On her chest she wore a pendant that attracts the eyes of men, and on her arm a gold wristband. In her hand she carried a wand of lapis lazuli.

'If I do not return in three days,' Inanna said to her minister Ninshubur, 'cry out for me in the cities and mourn for me in the temples. Tear at your cheeks and your breast; dress in a single garment like a beggar. Go to Enlil. Go to Nanna. Go to the temple of father Enki and weep before him. Enki is the god of wisdom. He knows the food of life and the water of life, and he will not let me die.' Then she turned towards the Underworld, and coming to the outer gates she knocked and said rudely, 'Open this door, Neti. I demand to enter.'

Neti, gatekeeper of the Underworld, reported to his queen, Inanna's sister Ereshkigal, that there was a visitor at the outer gate: 'A young woman as tall as Heaven stands at the gate.'

Ereshkigal bit her lip. Eventually she said: 'Impose on her the customs of the Underworld.'

So Neti returned to the outer gate. As Inanna entered, the crown of the land between the rivers was removed from her head.

'Why so?' said Inanna indignantly, and they said to her:

'Silence, Inanna. The customs of the Underworld are as they are, and may not be questioned.'

She went forward to the second gate, and demanded entrance. As she entered, the necklace of lapis lazuli beads was taken from her, and to her question the same reply was given. At the third gate, the band that crossed between her breasts was taken from her. At the fourth, the pendant that drew men's eyes was taken from her chest. At the fifth, the gold ring was taken from her wrist. At the sixth, the wand was taken from her hand. At the seventh, the royal robe was removed from her body.

'Why so?' said Inanna for the last time, and they answered her just as before.

Stark naked and bowing low, not unlike Psyche before the angry Venus, she entered the palace where Ereshkigal was enthroned. Inanna stepped forward as if to appeal to her sister, but the seven judges of the Underworld prevented her passage. They considered her for a moment and then turned the eye of death upon her. Inanna, like any other criminal, was hung on a meathook in the palace of Ereshkigal.

Ninshubur had not forgotten her. He went first to the temple of Enlil and wept before the god.

'Father Enlil,' he said, 'do not let precious metal be covered with the dust of death! Do not let fragrant wood be cut into planks for the carpenter! Do not let young Inanna die in the Underworld!'

'Young Inanna, queen here above, expected equal honour there below,' said Enlil. 'One who has braved the destiny of the Underworld does not return.'

Father Nanna gave the same answer. But when father Enki, the god of wisdom, heard Ninshubur's plea, he took dirt from under his fingernails and moulded two creatures of the insect kind, the Kurgarru and the Galaturru. Enki instructed them:

'Go and pester queen Ereshkigal. She will offer you food and drink; you must demand the carcass that hangs on the meathook.'

The Kurgarru and the Galaturru flew through the cracks of the gates of the Underworld. Ereshkigal was irritated by their buzzing, and said:

'Be quiet! Here is water to drink, a river clear and brim-full.'

'Not enough,' said the Kurgarru and the Galaturru.

'Here is bread to eat, the grain-fields ripe in summer.' But they were not satisfied. 'What else can I give you?' Ereshkigal demanded.

'That carrion hanging on the meathook,' said the two insects. 'We shall eat the flesh and drink the blood of it.'

Ereshkigal gave them Inanna's carcass. The Kurgarru scattered the food of life on Inanna's body, and the Galaturru sprinkled it with the water of life, and Inanna, the love goddess, was revived. She began to walk uphill; but no one is permitted to return from the Underworld without leaving another in her place. As she reached the outer gate, therefore, the bird-demons of the Underworld prevented her escape. The small demons held her by the legs and arms, the large demons held her by the shoulders and hair.

Outside the gate Ninshubur waited for his mistress, his cheeks and lips and chest lacerated by his own fingernails in the extremity of his grief. He threw himself on the ground in despair. 'You may go home, then, and we shall take Ninshubur in your place,' the demons laughed.

'No, not Ninshubur! It was through him that my life was returned to me.'

'Then we shall take Dumuzi in your place,' the demons said, and Inanna saw a vision of her husband Dumuzi, sitting enthroned beneath an apple tree at Uruk, playing on a shepherd's pipe. As she watched, demons armed with whips and axes seized him by his legs and arms. They broke the pipe that he was playing; they beat him with their whips, wounded him with their axes, and dragged him through the outer gate into the Underworld. He was led past her and onward into the dark city.

Not only had Inanna failed to conquer the Underworld: she had returned from it only in exchange for Dumuzi. The world could not do without him, however, and at New Year, by the favour of the sun god Utu, Inanna's brother, Dumuzi was reborn. Ever since then, so the Sumerians said, Dumuzi must spend a part of every year in the Underworld. Every spring the reborn Dumuzi watches over the revival of fruit trees and the frolicking of lambs and kids; he watches the fruit swell and the young animals gain in size and vigour; in high summer he sees the fruit picked, the young animals killed and the world turn dry and brown, and he himself is consigned to death once again.

In the literature of the Assyrians and Babylonians a similar story was told of Ishtar, the queen of Heaven, and Tammuz, the god who dies and is reborn every year, but it was motivated differently: so far from consigning Tammuz to the Underworld in the summer, Ishtar, it seems, was the one who rescued him at New Year. The Akkadian poet adds that once Ishtar had set off on her journey to the Underworld, *no bull mounted a cow, no donkey impregnated a jenny, No boy made love to a girl in the street: The boy slept alone in his room, the girl slept lying on her side;* the sexual act had ceased to be performed. Papsukkal, minister of the gods, noticed this disaster even before three days had elapsed. It was he who put on mourning clothes and stood before the god Ea, his father, with hair uncombed and beard untrimmed. On Papsukkal's persuasion, Ea created a creature who would distract Ereshkigal, thus making possible the release and reviving of Ishtar.

Throughout Mesopotamia, the women who lived in the temples of Ishtar and were dedicated to prostitution in honour of the love goddess had the particular duty, every year, of raising the lament for Tammuz, a lament in which they were led by the god's sister Belili. Other women joined them: the womenfolk of the exiled Israelites, to the disgust of their prophets, were among those who made offerings to the Queen of Heaven and joined in the annual lament for her dead husband Tammuz.

Every year these laments touched the heart of Ereshkigal, and Tammuz was permitted to return at New Year to the world above. Then, once more, the world became green with new leaves, bright with blossom and lively with the gambolling of lambs and kids. On the day of his annual return even the dead are privileged to rise and to smell the smoke of incense on the altars of the gods.

The Greeks, and after them the Romans, had their own views of Adonis (their name for Tammuz who was also Dumuzi). Most people made him out to be the child of a young Cypriot woman, Smyrna, who had slept with her own father Kinyras, a king of Cyprus, son of Paphos and grandson of Pygmalion.

The story of Adonis's conception and birth is a very strange one. It is told most fully by the Roman poet Ovid, though Ovid is retelling traditional Greek stories.

If the love goddess has any true home on earth, it is Cyprus, where the Greeks said that she was born. It is possible that they said this because it was on Cyprus that they themselves learned to worship her; it may even have been in the Cypriot temples of the love goddess that the Greeks first encountered the custom of sacred prostitution. According to the story as Ovid tells it, there was a certain sculptor named Pygmalion who worked on Cyprus and was disgusted by the shameless acts that one might see performed in the temples there, acts that he attributed to the unbridled lustfulness of the whole female sex. He therefore did not marry; but while living this solitary life he began to carve a statue in ivory. He used no model; possibly this statue embodied the most beautiful features of the various young women he happened to have seen on his occasional reluctant visits to the temple of Venus. At any rate, as it assumed its final shape, it was more beautiful than any woman he had ever seen, and so realistic that it seemed to want to live and move. Pygmalion gazed in wonder at his own creation, and began to feel a passionate love for this human form. He would often run his hands over it, as if continually in doubt whether ivory or living flesh lay under his hands. He kissed it, imagining that it kissed him back. He embraced it, although careful never to be too enthusiastic in his embraces for fear that bruises might appear on the skin. He spoke to it, and used to bring it little gifts – sea-shells and amber beads and freshly picked flowers for its hair. He dressed it, of course, as people do with statues in temples, and adorned it with silver, gold and precious stones, though Pygmalion found himself thinking that however fine his statue looked in rich robes and costly jewellery, it looked better still without any covering or adornment whatever.

One night Pygmalion had gently laid his statue on a soft, yielding couch, with a comfortable pillow for its head; he had covered it with sheets of Tyrian purple. Next morning at dawn he went to the temple of Venus: it was her festival, the most popular event of the year in Cyprus. Among the press of the crowds, the lowing of the cattle as they were led to sacrifice, and the smoke of frankincense, Pygmalion quietly made his own offering at the altar of the love goddess and said to her:

'If it is true, as they say, that the gods can do anything they wish, may I ask to have as my own wife … ' He did not dare to say, even in his mind, what he really wanted, and instead completed his silent prayer by asking the goddess for '… one who is just like my ivory girl?' Venus, who was naturally present since it was her festival, not only heard his prayer but understood its hidden meaning.

When Pygmalion returned home he leant over the ivory girl as she lay on her couch and kissed her. The ivory lips seemed warm. He touched her breasts, and they seemed as soft as flesh. Could he be right?

Was he imagining it? He stroked her body once more, as he had done rather often in the past, and felt the yielding of her skin, the pulsing of her veins, the beating of her heart. He kissed her again, and her ivory face was suffused with the most beautiful pink blush. Her eyes opened and she looked at him.

Luckily, she liked what she saw. He named her Galatea, because even now her skin was almost as white as milk. They were married – Venus herself attended the wedding – and less than a year later she bore him their child, Paphos, after whom is named the city that stands where Venus herself once stepped ashore. Paphos ruled all of Cyprus, and his son Cinyras ruled the island after him. Cinyras married a woman named Cenchreis and they had a daughter, Smyrna.

Smyrna was almost as beautiful as her great-grandmother, and when she had grown to adolescence there were many many from Cyprus and the East who came to her father's court with the aim of marrying her. She did not care for any of them, because, secretly, Smyrna was in love with her own father. Some said that Cupid had caused this forbidden love with an arrow (but for his part Ovid denies that Cupid could have done such a thing) and some said that Venus had caused it, being angry with Smyrna either because she had claimed to be as beautiful as the love goddess, or because her mother had made the claim on her behalf. This idea could easily persuade us – it is one of the strange similarities between the story of Smyrna and that of Psyche – but it is hard to square with what Venus did later, as we shall see. Smyrna's incestuous feelings were certainly caused by some god, as all human emotions are: as to which god, and why, we must leave the matter undecided.

'Whom shall it be, Smyrna?' said her father.

'Someone like you,' was all that she would say in answer, and her father, charmed by this, answered without any awareness of what his words might mean:

'I trust you will always love me as much as you do now!'

Smyrna, despairing of ever being able to express her love openly and sensing the horror that her father would feel if he knew of it, went to her room and prepared to kill herself. She had made a noose, hung it from a beam, and put a stool beneath it, but before she had had time to do more her old nurse, who was still with her as her personal maid, entered unexpectedly and saw in a moment what was happening.

So the two of them talked for a long time, and at last Smyrna brought herself to admit what she felt. Her nurse, in whose eyes Smyrna could do no wrong, began to consider how the matter could be arranged.

It was easy enough. For the forthcoming festival of Ceres all the married women of Cyprus were preparing to gather at a shrine far off in the hills and conduct mystery rites. For nine days, observing ritual purity, they would not sleep in their husbands' beds. The opportunity was too good to miss, and the nurse went to Cinyras and whispered to him that there was a certain girl of good family who was very much in love with him. She wished to sleep with him, but secretly and in darkness, so that her identity could not be betrayed.

'How old is she?' said the king, and the nurse answered truthfully:

'Just the same age as your daughter!'

Cinyras was not unwilling for this to be arranged. That night, therefore, the nurse accompanied Smyrna in absolute darkness to her father's bedside and said:

'Take her, king! She is yours.'

And so Cinyras made love to the girl, taking her virginity. The act gave both of them so much pleasure that they repeated it, still in darkness, for several days while the festival of Ceres continued. As Ovid says, they may well have called one another 'Father' and 'Daughter', as, in Greek, an older man and a younger woman, talking together intimately, might naturally do. Eventually, one night, consumed by curiosity about his nocturnal visitor, the king kept a lamp beside his bed, and after their lovemaking he lit it. Then he understood everything in a moment, and the consciousness that his daughter had made him unknowingly perform the act of incest, an act that the gods have specifically forbidden to humanity, filled him with disgust and anger. He sprang up, sword in hand, ready to kill her; but outside his room no lights were lit, and Smyrna was now sufficiently familiar with the palace in darkness to make good her escape.

She took ship for the mainland, and there she wandered for several months, eventually turning her steps southwards and crossing the hot, dry country of Arabia until she reached the mountainous kingdoms that line the Indian Ocean. Here at last, weary of her life, she knelt down and prayed to Gaia, the Earth, who comprehends all things including incest, to be merciful to her.

'While I live,' she said, 'I pollute the living. If I die, I shall pollute the dead. Solve this problem for me, mother Earth,' and the moist, crumbly earth gathered around her toes, while her skin turned to bark, her arms to branches, and her fingers and her hair to fronds and leaves. Henceforward Smyrna no longer shared the life that humans and animals know, nor the death that is their usual fate: she had a share of immortality, of that special kind that is appropriate to the vegetable kingdom. She was now a tree of a new species that would ever afterwards be valued for its tears of aromatic resin. *It will be spoken of through all ages,* said Ovid prophetically. As he said this he was quite unaware that having been offered alongside gold and frankincense at the birth of Jesus (which was just fifteen years before Ovid wrote the *Metamorphoses*) myrrh was to gain the eternal fame that he predicted.

The myrrh tree, which is called *smyrna* in Greek, still grows only in this same region: on the southern edge of Arabia, on the facing shore that we call Somalia, and on the island of Socotra in the Indian Ocean.

Smyrna was pregnant with her father's child. When nine months had passed from the festival of Ceres, the time when he had unknowingly taken her to his bed, the myrrh tree showed clear evidence of the onset of labour: it was bent and distorted in its agony, it groaned as if in pain, and tears of myrrh flowed ever more freely from it. Lucina, the goddess who attends childbirth, knew what was needed in this case, and she helped the bark to split open so that from a hollow in the interior a child could emerge. This child, immortal like the myrrh tree from which he sprang, was named Adonis.

In his adolescence, Adonis, great-grandson of Galatea, was the most handsome youth in the world. Naturally, Venus was interested in him. Her close observation of this young immortal was noticed by other gods and goddesses, but much more disturbing to Venus than the amused regard of the Olympians was the accidental intervention of her own son, Cupid, in the matter. It happened in this way. Venus was picnicking, invisible to mortals, in a meadow across which Adonis was sure to pass, accompanied by a band of youngsters who used regularly to go hunting together. Cupid, her dutiful son, was with her. They watched the butterflies and listened to the unmistakable sound of hunting dogs in the distance. 'They are getting closer,' thought Venus, and she began to direct nearly all of her attention towards a path that emerged from the woods not far downhill from where she was lying: this was the path along which she felt sure that Adonis and his party would come. Cupid, having no interest in Adonis, reached out for a cup of cool nectar.

Suddenly a pack of dogs dashed out of the woods along this path, and Venus started. Cupid was thrown off balance by her sudden movement and fell forward just enough for the arrows to tip out of the quiver that he wore over his shoulder. None of this would have mattered but for the fact that one of the arrows grazed Venus's breast in its trajectory. And at that moment Adonis himself emerged from the trees in hot pursuit.

So there it was. With the scratch of Cupid's arrow, Venus ceased to look on Adonis merely as a young man sufficiently handsome to deserve her special attention. Instead, she was head over heels in love with him.

'Sorry,' said Cupid.

Venus did not speak. The meadow seemed to shimmer before her eyes, and the group of boys appeared to be swaying slowly, dreamily, across it. The love goddess had never been in love before. If she had observed that a god or man seemed promising as a sexual partner, Venus considered him, and, when the opportunity arose, tested him in practice. If he tested well, she repeated the test, with whatever variations their imaginations might suggest. If he performed badly, she lost interest in him forthwith. These chosen males were very much at risk of falling in love with her, of course, and her mischievous son ensured that many of them did, but Venus had no obligation to reciprocate. So it had been with Adonis, too, until this moment.

'He's a bit young yet, surely?' said Cupid in a matter-of-fact tone.

Venus turned to him and tried to think of an answer, but she could not get the image of Adonis out of her head. And now Cupid looked down and saw that there was a scratch on her breast. His arrow had even drawn a little blood. Too late, he realized what he had done.

'I'll just go and see whether they caught it,' said Venus vaguely.

In retrospect, it would have been a good idea if Cupid had followed her and attempted with a second arrow to instil, in Adonis's heart, love for Venus that would at least equal her love for him. Instead, discreetly, he left his mother to her pursuit. When she came up with Adonis the young huntsman was on his own: his friends had gone on ahead with the slaughtered deer, while he was allowing his dogs a drink from a woodland stream.

Adonis was startled to see a beautiful young woman, quite alone, approaching through the woods.

'I am Venus, and I have lost my way among these trees,' said Venus. 'Which way are you going? May I go with you?'

Though startled, he was not very interested. Adonis had no time for girls; nor boys, for that matter. Hunting was what engaged his attention.

'I'm feeling rather tired,' said Venus. 'You won't be angry if I lean on your shoulder?' And shortly afterwards she added: 'I'm quite exhausted. Would you mind if we lay down here on the grass for a while?'

'I don't want to be out long,' Adonis observed. 'My friends will be worried about me.'

'Your arms feel so strong,' said Venus. 'Put them around me. I'm cold.'

How long was the courtship of Venus and Adonis? No Greek poet even suggests an answer. Shakespeare, who tells in *Venus and Adonis* the story that I am summarizing here, fits all but the final episode into a single day. Ovid, who told it before him, makes it clear that his Venus had plenty of time to become obsessively interested in hunting – the only way to Adonis's heart, if in fact there was any way.

> *She holds on to him* [says Ovid]. *She becomes his best friend.*
> *Accustomed to lounge in the shade and make herself beautiful,*
> *Venus now ranges the hills, the woods and the rocky ridges*
> *With her skirt turned up to her knees like Diana.*
> *She whistles up the dogs and goes after such animals as are safe*
>   *to hunt:*
> *Timid hares, antlered stags, roe deer …*

Poor Venus, in Ovid's story, did her very best to be one of the boys. Did she ever succeed, as a result, in persuading Adonis to make love to her? Ovid does not quite say. Shakespeare (who dedicates his poem to his good friend the earl of Southampton) seems certain that no such consummation ever took place.

'I definitely have to go now,' said Adonis.

'Help me up, then,' said Venus, and somehow in her clumsiness she managed to pull Adonis down on top of her. Having got this far, she kissed him. Then she kissed him again. 'I'm uncomfortable,' said Adonis. 'You really must let me go.'

'Let's meet again tomorrow.'

'No, I can't. That's exactly why I mustn't be late in bed tonight,' said Adonis. 'I need plenty of sleep. My friends and I are going after a wild boar tomorrow.'

Venus – both Ovid's Venus and Shakespeare's Venus – recoiled in horror. 'You must not do that! Big game is quite different from stags or hares. A boar can kill with its tusks; a lion's fangs and claws are just as deadly.' And according to Ovid (or rather, according to the legendary poet Orpheus, in whose mouth Ovid inserts these various stories of Pygmalion, Smyrna and Adonis) Venus at this point persuaded Adonis to lie comfortably on the grass, rested her head in his lap, kissed him several times more, and told him a story to explain her dislike for lions. Shakespeare, for his part, never lets them get quite so comfortable.

'There was once a young woman named Atalanta,' said Venus.

'Perhaps you have heard of her. She was the fastest runner of her day and also the most beautiful girl, and she asked Apollo's view concerning her future marriage. The god said to her in response:

"Atalanta, you have no need for a husband. Do not take one!
By marrying you will lose your own self."'

'Atalanta was frightened by this oracle. From that time on she lived only for the solitary pursuits of the forest – like you, Adonis – and when men came to court her she imposed a strange test on them.

"I am not to be possessed unless beaten in a race.
These are the rules. The man who defeats me
Shall have me; all losers will die."'

'It was a dangerous challenge; yet she was so very beautiful that many men were prepared to take it up, and a race was announced. Among the strangers who came to watch was a certain Hippomenes. He, like others, was ready to laugh at the contenders for their foolhardiness. Then he saw Atalanta's face; then he watched her strip for the race. Believe me, her figure when lightly clad was as lovely as mine, Adonis, or as yours would be if you were a girl! "Now I understand," said Hippomenes to himself. "Now I see what the prize will be. Perhaps I should try for it myself. God favours the brave, they say." While this went through his mind the race began, and Atalanta looked even more beautiful when she was racing, with her light garments pressed against her body or streaming behind her, and with her skin blushing in the cool air. She won the race. She was crowned with the olive wreath of victory, and each of her opponents in turn submitted to the sacrificial axe. Then Hippomenes stepped forward and challenged her, and of all the men she had so far encountered he was the only one about whom she began to wonder whether it might be a good idea to let him win. Meanwhile,' Venus continued, 'Hippomenes prayed to me.

"Goddess of Cythera, be with me.

You lit this fire. Make it blaze!'"

'As it happened I was present in person: I wanted to see the race quite as much as Hippomenes did, so I had arrived from Cyprus that very day. The finest apples in the world grow in the orchards of Tamasus on Cyprus, and I had brought three of them with me. So I went over to Hippomenes (no one else could see me, of course), gave them to him, and told him what to do. Then they began to race, just the two of them this time. Although tired, and not so enthusiastic as in the earlier race, Atalanta still managed to increase her lead over Hippomenes gradually, until the moment when he rolled the first of the apples ahead of him across her path. It looked so lovely that she turned off her course enough to catch it and pick it up. Hippomenes meanwhile passed her. But she soon rallied and overtook him once more. So he rolled another apple, and the same thing happened again. Then, with his last apple, Hippomenes prayed to me a second time:

"You gave me this apple, goddess: be with me now!'"

'He threw this third apple further off the course, so that she had to follow it into the long grass. After this delay – and now carrying three lovely big apples – she couldn't regain the lead. Hippomenes was crowned victor, and led Atalanta away as his prize.'

'They loved one another very much. But he did not trouble to thank me, and he burned not one tear of frankincense on my altar. So, soon afterwards, when he and Atalanta were walking together and were passing Cybele's shrine, I made them want to have sex. They went into the sanctuary and coupled there shamelessly against the temple wall. Cybele was so angry at this sacrilege that she turned them into lions and yoked them to her chariot. This transformation was a harsh punishment for their lustfulness because, as you surely know, lions never mate with one another: a lion mounts a leopardess, while a lioness submits to a male leopard. So Hippomenes and Atalanta now range the wildest forests of Greece, roaring with anger and desire: they are unable ever again to perform the sexual act together. Their frustration explains why lions are the most dangerous of all animals (unless bridled and yoked to Cybele's chariot), and boars are the next fiercest after lions. And apart from all that, don't you realize that I'm in love with you?' Venus ended. 'If only for my sake, don't hunt big game. I can't bear to think of you tomorrow, at risk of being wounded by a boar or mauled by a lion.'

'I don't think it's love,' said Adonis roughly. 'You just want me like Atalanta wanted Hippomenes, and I haven't time; and this sex business is all your own fault, if you're the goddess Venus. Anyway, sex talk makes me blush.' With that, he wriggled out of her arms for the last time and ran for home.

Next morning Venus was out early in her chariot, drawn through the sky by white swans, listening once more for the sound of hunting dogs. It was not long before she heard them, but something in the note seemed at once to confirm her fears. Surely that was a howl of mourning, not the wild barking of a hunt in progress? She put the question out of her mind and descended to earth in a forest glade. Striding from there towards the sound of the dogs, she heard a hunstsman whistling them up. That was Adonis, she thought; I know his whistle. But she was wrong. As the trees opened out, she saw something that would always be etched into her memory – Adonis himself, lying white and motionless, with a great, bloody gash along the side of his body, and his friends helplessly watching him die.

It was said by some afterwards that the pomegranate tree, whose fruits are known for their red juice, first grew from the blood shed by Adonis.

Such events do not happen without a divine cause. Why did Adonis meet his fatal boar?

Various suggestions are made by Greek authors. It was easy for them to suppose that Artemis (Diana, as Ovid would have called her) had caused the incident: she is the goddess of the hunt, after all. We then have to pursue the question one step backwards and ask why Artemis would have done it. The only likely answer is that she was angry with Venus for attempting to seduce Adonis and to distract him from the sexless enthusiasm for hunting which he shared with Artemis. Since she was unable to punish Venus directly – the two goddesses were fairly equally matched – she had to assuage her anger by destroying the object of Venus's love. This is possible, certainly. It is at least equally possible that Ares intervened in the matter: he certainly could have sent the boar in Adonis's direction. His motive will be even more obvious. Like Hephaistos before him, Ares had by now sufficient reason to be jealous, if jealousy is of any real use in a relationship with Venus. Lacking the nerve to take out his anger on Venus, Ares might well have made Adonis his target instead, just as Artemis might have done. Whichever of these two was his divine enemy, Adonis personally had not deserved the enmity, having given Venus as little encouragement as a young man can.

There is also a quite different story as to why Adonis died, and it is told by several Greek authors. They say that Venus was not, as a matter of fact, the only goddess who had noticed him. His youthful beauty had also been observed by Persephone, queen of the Underworld. Both of them were sure that although Adonis was at present only interested in hunting, this was bound to change as he progressed through adolescence. The two goddesses quarrelled and possibly fought over the right to the long-term possession of Adonis. They could find no other way of settling their dispute, so they asked Zeus to decide for them.

'How can I possibly judge between you?' said Zeus in exasperation. 'You are both so perfectly beautiful. The poor boy himself is bound to believe that he is in love with whichever of you has inveigled him into bed at the time. Very well: this is how it must be. Venus, you shall have him for four months of every year, the spring and early summer months when the world is green and even Adonis's fancy will eventually turn to thoughts of love. Persephone, he shall be yours for the winter, when the world is cold. He can keep warm and keep you warm beside the fires of the Underworld. But you two insatiable goddesses must remember that Adonis has other, more manly interests too. He doesn't want to spend all his time with females. He shall have four months of each year to himself, the late summer and autumn. At that season he can go hunting as often as he likes.'

So it was decided, and the wild boar that killed Adonis was sent to him by the Fates, late that same autumn, because there was no other way in which Zeus's decree could be put into effect.

Venus herself, since she was at hand when he died, took part in his funeral, and herself placed his body in a wooden chest with spices and aromatic resins to preserve it from all corruption. In obedience to Zeus's command, she sent this chest to Persephone in the Underworld, and Adonis spent his next four months among the dead (of whom he was one) in Persephone's company. It was said by some that when four months had passed, and it was time for Persephone to give Adonis back, she refused. That could be why, in Greek myth, Venus encourages the women who are her slaves or pay her special honour, notably the prostitutes in her temples, to raise the lament for Adonis every spring.

Thus the women succeed in frustrating Persephone's selfish plan; and somehow it is once again Venus, with the help of her own slaves and devotees, who gets what she wants. Adonis in Greek and Roman mythology, like Dumuzi and Tammuz in the Near East, is reborn every year as the fresh green leaves begin to show and the lambs and kids are thriving in their pastures. An ancient commentator on the poems of Theokritos was among the first to say clearly that the winter period during which Adonis is in the Underworld corresponds precisely to the farming winter during which the grain is not yet visible above ground. Ever dying, ever revived, he is a strangely weak and unmanly figure – a lettuce-eater who is now as happy to lie with Venus's head in his lap as to go hunting for boars; but Venus has other, more vigorous lovers if she needs them. It is at least an indication of her success that Adonis spends with Venus not only the four months that Zeus originally decreed, but also the four months of late summer and autumn during which Zeus allowed him his freedom.

5

The Events on Mount Ida

ZEUS WAS OFTEN DISPLEASED BY THE MISCHIEVOUS GAMES OF VENUS, WHICH regularly set the Olympians quarrelling. He was most especially annoyed by the claims she liked to make concerning how many times she had got the other gods and goddesses tangled up in sexual affairs with mortals. He himself was among her victims. As the ancient *Hymn to Aphrodite* says,

> *She turns aside the thought even of Zeus whose delight is thunder,*
> *Whose nature it is to be greatest, who holds the greatest honour;*
> *Even his strong mind she beguiles whenever she wishes*
> *And easily makes him join in love with mortal women*
> *Deceiving Hera, his sister and wife.*

It seems to me, Zeus thought, that golden Venus herself is the only Olympian who has been exempt from the humiliation of a mortal love affair. Well, why should it be so? Why should she not suffer like the rest?

With the king of the gods, to think is to act. We remember that this is how Zeus decided, no more than a moment after the idea had first popped into his head, to marry Venus to Hephaistos. Such snap decisions brought unexpected consequences, no doubt, but meanwhile they added excitement to divine life.

Zeus now made another snap decision. He would teach Venus a lesson. He would bring home to her the serious consequences of these games that she liked to play with the affections of their fellow

Olympians. How? That would be easy. With the help of Eros he would make her fall in love with a mortal herself. Zeus knew of so many mischievous things that Eros had done, many of which had never yet been reported to his mother, that he had an unbreakable hold over the young god of love. If Zeus wanted something, Eros had no choice but to supply it.

Together, Zeus and Eros worked on their conspiracy. They both wanted to give her a handsome lover. Eros wanted this because he felt he owed it to his mother, whom he was guiltily aware that he was deceiving. Zeus wanted it for aesthetic reasons: if you are going to watch a pair of lovers at work, they might as well be beautiful. Now the handsomest mortal at this moment was Anchises, who belonged to a noble family that owned lands in the neighbourhood of the famous city of Troy. Young Anchises seemed to have no emotional entanglements, and was at present sharing the task of keeping his family's herds of cattle on the slopes of Mount Ida where many springs rise, Ida the mother of wild creatures – the mountain mass that rises to the southeast of Troy.

So Eros, on some excuse, persuaded his mother to glance at Mount Ida, and while she was looking for whatever object of mild interest he was pointing to, he easily found the opportunity to loose an arrow at her heart. She did not even feel it.

> *Then smile-loving Aphrodite caught sight of Anchises*
> *And wanted him: vast desire took hold of her heart* [says the *Hymn*].

The arrows of Eros never kill, but they always find their mark.

Having told us of the moment when Venus's eyes first rested on Anchises, the poet of the ancient *Hymn* next explains how she made ready to seduce him.

> *She went to Cyprus and entered her aromatic temple*

At Paphos, where is her precinct and aromatic altar.
There she closed the gleaming doors
And the Graces washed her and rubbed her with oil
Ambrosial …

This was the oil, perfumed with the costliest, most exotic aromas of the Orient, that prepared Venus's body for love. If she was to meet Anchises on the hillside of Ida, however, even Venus needed clothes – a filmy shift next to her skin; after that,

… a robe brighter than the glow of fire,
Fair, golden, all decorated: like the moon
It shone over her tender breasts, wonderful to see.
She had twisted brooches and bright shell-earrings
And beautiful circlets around her tender neck.

Thus adorned, Venus flew off from Cyprus and made her way among the clouds to Mount Ida, where she alighted in the forest not far from Anchises' mountain cabin. As she strode through the forest, grey wolves, tawny lions, bears and swift leopards gathered about her, fawning, and she regarded them with proprietorial pleasure, and put desire for one another in their hearts, and they crept away, two by two, to their shady lairs and lay down together pleasurably.

It was convenient for Venus that the other herdsmen who worked with Anchises, tending his family's cattle, were away in the fields. It was his rest period, and he was alone in the cabin which they all shared, pacing the floor as he practised on his lyre.

He heard the soft footsteps of a woman in the yard and stood at the door. Venus approached. She had made herself look like a young unmarried mortal woman, but he was still fascinated by her fine robe, her jewellery and the perfect beauty of her face.

'Greetings, lady,' said Anchises. 'You are surely one of the gods, Artemis, Leto, maybe Venus or Themis or grey-eyed Athene; maybe one of the Graces, who attend on all the gods and are said to be immortal, or a nymph of forest or mountain or water-meadow. Whoever you are, I will build you an altar on a high peak, and offer sacrifices to you in every season. In return, lady, be favourable to me; grant that I may be famous among the Trojans, long-lived, happy among my people, and fortunate in my descendants!'

'I am not a goddess,' Venus lied to him. 'I am mortal, daughter of Otreus king of Phrygia: you must have heard of him. But I can speak your language too, because I had a Trojan nurse. A strange thing has happened to me. We were dancing, nymphs and mortal women together, dancing for Artemis who carries a golden staff, and a numberless crowd stood round us watching. Then suddenly I was carried off by the dog-killer, by Hermes the god of thieves, away from the dance, across many fields where mortal men drive their oxen and across wide lands that lie unploughed and unclaimed, roamed by wild flesh-eating beasts. He carried me through the air – my feet did not even touch the ground. He brought me to your mountain pastures, Anchises, and told me that I was fated to turn from virgin girl to married woman in your bed, and that I would bear you fine children. So take me, a girl as yet untamed and unpractised in love, to your father and mother and brothers, and prepare for our wedding and the time when we shall be united in love.'

Anchises considered this, and considered the young woman who stood before him.

'Well, if you are mortal, and your parentage is as you say, and the Olympian god Hermes brought you here to me and told you that you were to be my wife … Well, then, no god, and no mortal man either, is going to stand in my way. I shall make love to you now, this very day. Even if far-shooting Apollo himself were to threaten me with the deadly arrows from his silver bow, and death and the Underworld were to be my punishment, I would still take you to my bed.'

With these words he took her firmly by the hand. Smiling Venus, who had known very well that this would happen, followed him with a nice show of reluctance, wriggling this way and that as if trying to escape, blushing and looking down at the ground with those beautiful eyes. It made no difference. He led her into the mountain hut and to his bed, spread with blankets and draped with the skins of bears and lions that he himself had hunted and killed in the mountains of Ida.

And when they had climbed into his well-made bed
He took the shining jewellery from her body,
Pins and twisted brooches and shell-earrings and necklaces,
Undid her belt, took off her bright clothes
And placed them on a silver-studded stool;
Then Anchises, by the will of the gods and by destiny,
Bedded with her – a mortal with a goddess, unawares.

This is the story told in the *Hymn to Aphrodite*, and it is a strange one. It is true that Anchises carried out this dangerous act *unawares*, meaning that he did not know that his sexual partner was an immortal. But it is also true that he deserved to have known, and that he was deceived.

Afterwards, when Anchises lay in his bed satisfied, Venus poured sweet sleep over his eyes. At her leisure she dressed, put on her jewellery once more, and assumed her true divine size and beauty. Her head touched the roof beams of his little mountain hut, and her face shone like a star, the wandering star that is generally named after Venus or Aphrodite. Then, kneeling beside him on the bed, she touched his shoulder to wake him, and said:

'Get up, son of Dardanos! Why are you so sleepy? Now look at me, and answer me this: do you think I still look the same as when you first saw me approaching you through the forest?'

Now, too late, Anchises knew for certain who she was. He crouched down in terror, hid his face in the blankets, and reached out to clasp her legs in supplication. He said to her:

'As soon as I saw you, Venus, I guessed you were an immortal; but you lied to me and told me otherwise. I know well that men who have performed the act of love with a goddess suffer for it afterwards: people say that they live the rest of their lives weak-kneed, cloudy-eyed, half-witted. Pity me! I am your suppliant before Zeus. As I lie humbly at your feet, as I clasp your divine knees, promise me that you will not make me live my life in that condition.'

'Anchises,' Venus said to him soothingly, 'do not be so frightened! You must not fear my displeasure unduly, nor that of the other gods. I can tell you that your earlier prayers will be fulfilled. When I first came to you, you asked me to make you famous among your people and fortunate in your offspring. It shall be so. Together we will have a fine son: he will be a king among the Trojans, and he will have descendants, son following son without interruption. I find it strange, however, that you did not ask me for immortality, as you might have done.'

'I never imagined that immortality was available,' he said.

'You were wise not to think of it. Immortality is a two-edged gift. You know the name of Ganymede?'

'Of course I do,' said Anchises. 'He was the son of Tros, and was stolen from this very hillside.'

'He was taken by Zeus to be his boyfriend,' said Venus, 'the form of love over which I do not preside. Well, Ganymede is now immortal and ageless. This means that he will never become a man: he himself will never taste the pleasures of love. He will never persuade a girl to love him; he can never take the man's role in the sexual act. He will always be a boy, doomed to be the passive object of Zeus's lust for ever.

'And you have surely heard what became of Tithonos? He also was a Trojan, and his story is even more painful. Eos, the goddess of the dawn, who with her rosy fingers brings light to the eastern sky, fell in love with him. I know she did: I made her do it because I was angry with her. In the foolishness that love often brings, she went from his bed to the throne of Zeus, king of the gods, and asked him for half a favour. "Make Tithonos immortal, father Zeus," she said. And so he did. Eos did not ask for the gift of agelessness, of eternal youth, to be enjoyed alongside the first; so Zeus did not grant it.'

'What happened to Tithonos was this. As long as he was a handsome young man he lived with Eos in her house beside the streams of Oceanos at the edge of the world, and they were happy. But when the first grey hairs began to appear on his handsome head, and there was grey mixed in with the black of his beard, Eos no longer wished him to share her bed, though he still lived in her palace and ate ambrosia and drank nectar with her, and she still provided him with immortal garments and sewed his buttons on. Eventually old age oppressed him so that he could no longer move or lift his limbs, the limbs whose vigour once attracted her desire. Eos decided that there was now only one thing left for her to do. She put him away in one of the rooms of her house beside the Ocean, and she closed the door. There his voice still flows on endlessly, but he is no longer able to move. That is how it will be for him until the end, if there is any end.'

'If those are the forms of immortality that are available to mortals,' said Anchises, 'I don't wish for either of them.'

'And you will not have them. Instead, sickness and death will come to you as to all other mortals, to exhaust you, weaken you and eventually kill you. Yet your family will be closer than all others to the immortal gods.'

'What will become of our son, then?'

'I will entrust him to the Nymphs, Anchises, to the full-breasted Nymphs of Mount Ida. They will nurture him in his infancy. When he is five years old I will bring him to you again, and you will be proud of him. You may tell people that he is the son of a Nymph with whom you slept one night in a forest glade. We shall name your son Aeneas, a name that will remind me of my shame.'

'You need feel no shame ...' Anchises began.

'You know nothing about it. The other goddesses will laugh at me for submitting to a mere man. I shall no longer be able to tease them, at dinner on Mount Olympos, by reminding them of their misbehaviour. I shall have to stop making fun of the gods who have lusted for mortal girls and have fathered bastard children on them, because now, thanks to one of them – and whichever it was, my wicked son surely helped him – I have fallen into the trap that I so often set for others. I have been very foolish.'

'Need they know?' said Anchises.

'Can you keep it secret?' Venus asked him. 'When young men are drinking wine together and talking about girls, can you hold your tongue?'

'Of course,' he said angrily.

'Then you will save me from shame and you will save yourself from Zeus's anger,' said Venus. 'It is true, as you said, that men who make love with goddesses often suffer for it afterwards. If you can keep our secret, then I think I will visit you again ….'

Venus thought it better not to admit to Anchises that she was unable to protect him from the king of the gods. He was fated to suffer Zeus's anger as other men had. The fact is that Zeus and Eros, as well as Helios, were watching with pleasure when Anchises took Venus to bed in his mountain hut, and when the entertainment was over Zeus said:

'I regret this, but it is my invariable rule to punish men who do such things with goddesses.'

'It's hard on him,' said Eros. 'He really had no choice. What would you have done in his place?'

'The same,' said Zeus, 'and the Fates, or Hera, would have punished me too, though less severely. Well, I will be lenient. I will allow him to enjoy his youth and strength to the full.'

Many years afterwards, when Aeneas was grown up and was one of the princes of Troy, and Anchises no longer went with his herdsmen to the mountain pastures, Zeus did at last strike him with lightning. It was commonly supposed that at some time during those intervening years Anchises had broken his word to Venus by telling a confidential friend about their secret affair and about the true parentage of Aeneas. In fact that really had nothing to do with it, because there had never been a secret: Zeus knew all the time and Helios had long since told the story to everyone on Mount Olympos. But it allowed Anchises to believe, through the terrible years of the Trojan War and the flight to Italy – the years after the fateful lightning strike, when Anchises lived on, weakened and unable to walk – that he had brought this punishment on himself. It was better thus, Venus knew, than that he should wonder whether Venus, his divine lover from long ago and the mother of his son, had broken her word.

There was a theory that Zeus planned the Trojan War so that Helen, his own mortal daughter by Leda, would have the fame of setting Europe and Asia at loggerheads; and in favour of this it must be said that from the beginning of history to the end of 2004 not one of the recorded causes of war has been as beautiful as Helen. There was a second theory, which may be characterized as geomythical, that Zeus and Themis, the goddess who personifies justice, planned the Trojan War together as a way of relieving the earth of the ever-growing multitude of humanity. There was a third theory: because Tyndareos, once king of Sparta, customarily sacrificed to all the gods except Venus, she decided to make all the daughters of Tyndareos and Leda 'twice-married and thrice-married and abandoners of their husbands'; against this, Venus knew very well that Tyndareos was not Helen's father, and if she wanted to get Helen into trouble could have done so with less earth-shattering consequences than by promising her to Paris.

There was even a fourth theory, and this one also looks to Venus as the cause. The love goddess herself planned the Trojan War, it is said, so that a child of hers – her son Aeneas – would found a ruling dynasty and a world empire.

If this was her plan, it was a complicated one. The first step was taken at the marriage of the sea-goddess Thetis to the mortal Peleus, who was king of Iolkos in northern Greece. Their wedding feast was a great event, attended by gods, mortals and centaurs. It is described in many sources, but only one incident is relevant to the present story. The sister and best friend of Ares, the goddess Eris, whose name means 'Discord', is usually left off the guest list at weddings, but on this occasion, possibly owing to a hint from Venus, she came anyway. She caused no quarrel between the newly married pair. Instead she took a ripe apple, scratched some words on it and rolled it into the middle of the circle of women and goddesses gathered around the bride. One of them picked it up and read the inscription: 'For the most beautiful'.

'It must be meant for me,' said Hera, Athene and Venus, all speaking at once.

Why an apple? Adonis might well have interrupted to ask this question when he was listening to the story of Atalanta and Hippomenes. It was said that in the mythological past the first apple tree had been a gift of grandmother Gaia to Zeus and Hera at their wedding; among the Sumerians, Inanna had been the owner of apple trees in the first orchard on Earth. Apples were gifts between married couples in many myths and in everyday life, and they carried a magical power which was just as useful before marriage and outside it: if you could make a member of the opposite sex pick up an apple and – most especially – suck its juices, that person would unfailingly be yours.

In the present case, either as a piece of random mischief or by Venus's plan, Eris had misused an apple at a wedding to cause not love but discord. The three goddesses appealed to Zeus to decide between them, but they might have predicted that Zeus himself would refuse the challenge. He values his relationships with Athene and Venus, and he respects Hera's power to make his life uncomfortable.

'I cannot possibly judge between you,' said Zeus carefully, 'because I find you all equally beautiful, and, sadly, there is only one prize. None of the other gods would make a suitable judge; they know you too well, and are sure to be biased in favour of one or other of you. I have a young mortal in mind for the task. Hermes, I have work for you.'

Zeus instructed Hermes to take the apple, and the three goddesses, to Mount Gargaros in the Ida range, south of Troy.

'There you will find young Paris, herding his father's cattle. Trojans seem to do little else. Tell him he is to judge a beauty competition between Hera, Athene and Venus. Take this apple: it is the prize for the winner. Paris is a personable boy and I gather he is not unfamiliar with women, so he should have no difficulty with this commission.'

Paris was actually a prince of the royal line of Troy, one of the many children of king Priam and queen Hekabe, though Paris himself was unaware of the fact. During her pregnancy Hekabe had dreamed that she gave birth to a flaming torch. She was advised by those who interpret such omens that her baby must not be allowed to live. Soon after his birth, therefore, Paris was taken to Mount Ida and abandoned there. Some say that the tiny infant was suckled by a bear; certainly he was eventually found and rescued by a group of slave cowherds, among whom he grew up. Life among the mountain pastures of Troy had given him, as Zeus observed, sufficient opportunities for experiencing love, though most of his girl friends had been slaves like himself.

The Trojan lady Andromache – in Euripides's tragedy *Andromache* – says that the three goddesses prepared for their competition by bathing in an ice-cold stream high on Mount Ida. Perhaps she knew the truth. Others, by contrast, have supposed that they spent some time at home on Mount Olympos, with the aid of their usual attendants, perfecting their beauty with the help of perfumes, jewellery and fine clothing. The ancient poet who composed the epic *Kypria* asserted that when Venus emerged,

> *Her body was dressed in clothes that the Graces and Horai*
> *Made for her and dipped in as many fresh flowers*
> *As the seasons bear: in saffron and squill*
> *And spreading violet and the flower of the rose, fair*
> *And sweet and nectar-like, and the ambrosial buds*
> *Of narcissus … Thus Aphrodite*
> *Was dressed in clothes redolent of every season.*

This poet does not mention, but the Byzantine commentator Eustathios confidently guesses, that Venus wore her magical embroidered band *in which all enchantments were woven: love, desire and whispered words of love*. This, in itself, had Paris come under its spell, would have clinched her victory. She must have recalled, as she put it on, the famous occasion when Hera had asked to borrow it and had concealed the reason. 'I am visiting Okeanos and Tethys, at the edge of the world,' Hera had lied, 'because I want to stop them quarrelling. If Tethys wears your embroidered band Okeanos cannot fail to be dazzled by her beauty once again.' Venus had lent the precious object, and Hera had put it on herself, her real aim, all along, being to force Zeus to love her once again. Venus must also have wondered at the inconsistency shown by Athene, goddess of war and of the arts. Why should she, of all goddesses, trouble herself with a beauty competition? Hadn't she once caught Venus sitting at a loom, and complained that her own artistic province was being invaded? Venus had promised for the future to stick to love and beauty: now here was Athene herself invading that territory.

'This is mere idle curiosity, Hermes,' said Venus as the four of them trooped off towards Ida, 'but what do you know about Paris? Has he a wife?'

'Not a wife, exactly. He's seeing a mountain nymph, Oinone,' said Hermes. 'Of course these romances never last.'

'I wonder if he has ever wanted to be a soldier?' Athene mused.

'Oh, no. Somehow I feel sure he has political ambitions,' Hera said.

As they alighted on the summit of Mount Gargaros, Hera gave a little laugh and said, turning to Venus: 'You lead the way now, my girl. You must know all these footpaths, considering how often you used to hang around here. A mortal, wasn't it? Anchises?'

Deep inside herself Venus laughed as she thought of her son and his future.

'No, I'll go in front,' said Hermes, aware of the crackle of jealousy in the air. 'I know the way. In fact this is the very rock where Zeus and I found Ganymede playing his pipe.' Venus allowed herself a smile. Hera, who hated her husband's young cupbearer, subsided into furious silence.

The three goddesses walked in line behind Hermes. Suddenly, as they rounded a rocky outcrop, he spoke.

'Good day, cowherd! Paris, isn't it?'

'Who are you, then?' asked Paris. 'And who are those women with you?'

'They are not women, Paris,' said Hermes. 'They are Hera, Athene and Venus. Zeus requires you to choose the prizewinner in a beauty competition between them. It's nothing you're not used to, if you've judged cattle shows. This apple is the prize.'

Paris was not eager for the task. He immediately saw, as Zeus had seen before him, that the judge of such a competition would have made one friend but two enemies.

'You must not refuse Zeus's command,' said Hermes. 'Now will you judge them as you see them here, or do you require them to undress?'

'I'll see it all. I might as well be hung for a sheep as a lamb,' Paris replied, sweating slightly.

'You will have noticed, young man,' said Hera calmly as she

unclasped the brooch at her shoulder, 'that mortal poets tell the truth when they call me *white-armed*. You are about to see what the poets do not dare to imagine: the skin of my whole body is as white and smooth as that of my arms.'

'If I may make a suggestion, Paris,' said Athene, 'be sure that Venus takes off all her jewellery. Be careful of the embroidered band that crosses between her breasts.'

'I'll take it off when you take off your magic goatskin,' Venus replied. 'And your helmet, Athene. You'd strike terror into any ordinary young man. But I believe Paris is no ordinary young man,' and with that she allowed her shift to fall to her feet. At the astonishing sight of the three most beautiful of goddesses together, naked, on Mount Ida, in full daylight under the open sky, it is said that cockerels crowed and donkeys brayed and every bull mounted his favourite cow and every vine embraced its elm.

'I will consider you each in turn,' said Paris. 'Hera has precedence.'

Ox-eyed Hera (as the poets also called her) stepped forward, standing close enough to Paris to whisper: 'Choose me, young man, as I deserve, and I will make you the ruler of all of Asia.'

'I will judge impartially,' said Paris.

Athene came next, and as she approached Paris she said: 'In considering me, young Paris, you should know that though Ares is called the god of war, I am the one who fights and always wins. If you choose me, as I deserve, I will make sure that you never lose a battle.'

'You need have no concern. I will judge impartially,' said Paris.

Then Venus stepped forward, and Paris was amazed by her beauty. She stood very close to him, so that he was aware of the scent of her breath and the perfume of her body.

'Look at me carefully, master Paris. Notice the perfection of every detail. And while you are studying me, think about your forthcoming marriage ...'

Paris completed Venus's sentence: 'To a farm girl from across the valley there.'

'Wrong,' said Venus. 'To the most beautiful woman in the world – the only one who deserves to lie in your bed as your wife. Shall I tell you her name?'

'I will judge impartially,' said Paris mechanically. 'Tell me, then.'

'Helen, a child of Zeus. She is married to Menelaos: they are king and queen of Sparta. I will restore you to your proper position at Troy: you are a prince by birth, you know. I will guide you to Sparta, and I will steer Helen into your arms, if she needs steering. There is no other mortal who rivals my beauty as she does. Just look again at the contour of my breasts: could anything be more beautiful? Helen resembles me closely.'

Venus turned and walked slowly back towards her two rivals, leaving Paris to consider his verdict. He found it an easy decision, after all.

'The beauty of all three goddesses is beyond human measure,' Paris announced formally, 'but Zeus has instructed me to make a choice and I must not disobey. I award this apple, bearing the words "For the most beautiful", to Venus.'

Not long after this event a band of townsmen came from Troy and stole one of Paris's bulls. They needed an animal for sacrifice at an athletic competition, and this was the simplest way to get one.

Unable to challenge the thieves on his own, Paris followed them to Troy. Having seen his stolen bull slaughtered, he decided that at least he might as well compete in the races that followed. Among the competitors were several of the princes of Troy. These, unknown to Paris, were his own brothers. He won the race, and queen Hekabe, disturbed by the ominous victory of an unknown slave over her princely sons, consulted her daughter Kassandra on what action to take.

'He must be killed,' said the prophetess Kassandra.

So prince Deiphobos was ordered by Hekabe to kill Paris at the same altar at which his bull had been sacrificed. But as Deiphobos raised his axe to carry out this instruction, a young woman from the crowd stepped forward and said:

'Hekabe! King Priam! Do you know that this slave whom you are about to kill is your own son?'

She was sufficiently beautiful that the whole audience fell silent to hear what she had to say and to await the king and queen's response. She was, of course, Venus.

'Prove this claim if you can!' said Priam.

At Venus's command, Paris showed the jewels that had been left with him when he was exposed. Hekabe examined them carefully.

'It is true,' she said slowly. 'I can hardly believe it. Here are the necklace and pendant that I gave to my newborn son when they took him to the slopes of Mount Ida. I was instructed by the soothsayers to expose him, but I have never ceased to think about him. There can be no mistake.'

So Kassandra's advice was ignored, as would so often happen in the years that followed. Paris was welcomed back to the royal house of Troy, and in due course had the opportunity to make a journey to southern Greece.

Now Helen, wife of Menelaos and queen of Sparta, had an unusual origin. The story is variously told, but it is usually said that she and her brothers Kastor and Polydeukes were all three born from an egg, and that their father was Zeus, who had turned himself temporarily into a swan in order to seduce the goddess Nemesis, whose name means 'fate'. The egg, if produced by Nemesis, was hatched by Leda, the wife of king Tyndareos of Sparta, and some omit Nemesis from the story altogether, saying that Zeus's disguise was adopted in order to seduce Leda. It is further said that Leda had made love with her husband Tyndareos on the same night that Zeus appeared to her, and that Tyndareos, not Zeus, was the true father of one or both of the boys; but few doubt that Helen, in one way or another, was truly the child of Zeus.

As for Menelaos, he was the brother of Agamemnon, king at Mycenae. It was through his marriage to Helen that he had become king of Sparta. They welcomed prince Paris to Sparta and entertained him royally, but, while he was still their guest, Menelaos had to sail to Crete to take part in the funeral rites for his grandfather Katreus, one of the sons of Minos.

When Paris first saw queen Helen, enthroned with her husband, presiding over the banquet that was held to celebrate his own arrival, he knew instantly that this was the woman for him. As for Helen, she fell in love with him at once. She did not want to, but she was unable to resist, and she did not know why. Some later Greeks said unkindly that Helen had been eager to be seduced, but the real reason for her behaviour is clear: Venus's wicked son Eros was behind her, driving her into the arms of Paris. Helen chose the pain of betraying her husband rather than the pain of resisting Eros.

Already weakened by the turmoil in her heart, Helen found that she could not bear to be alone once Menelaos had left for Crete. She had to talk, and Paris was ready to listen. Soon it was as if she had never had any other confidant. Long before her dilatory husband had set out on his return voyage, Helen had packed her own valuables, and as many of Menelaos's as she could lay hands on, into Paris's ships, and they were off, accompanied only by an old servant woman of Helen's; her daughter, the nine-year-old Hermione, she left behind. After the first day's sailing they put in at Kranae. It was during that night, according to many sources, that Paris and Helen first made love; but there was also a more prosaic and more scandalous story, that they had already gone to bed together in Menelaos's house. The other events of their journey are hardly part of this story: were they beset by storms off Cyprus and did they sail on to Sidon in Phoenicia? Did Paris kill the king of Sidon, their host, and kidnap a group of skilled Phoenician weavers to be handmaidens to Helen? They arrived, eventually, at Troy, and their wedding was held on Mount Ida, where, according to the poet of the epic *Kypria*, *smile-loving Aphrodite* was in attendance with her usual entourage:

> *Weaving fragrant garlands, flowers of the earth,*
> *The goddesses with shining veils put them on their heads –*
> *The Nymphs and Graces, and golden Aphrodite with them,*
> *Singing beautifully on Ida, mountain of many springs.*

Meanwhile in Crete, Menelaos had been preparing to leave for home when the news reached him of Helen's elopement. It was brought by Iris, the goddess of the rainbow, who had seen Paris and Helen embarking together in the morning mists. Learning on his return that he had lost not only a beautiful wife but also a chest of gold and precious stones, Menelaos took advice on the best course of action. Since Paris was a prince of the powerful city of Troy, retrieving Helen would have to be a matter of diplomacy or perhaps war. The advice of his neighbour to the west, Nestor, the venerable king of Pylos, was philosophical:

Wine, Menelaos, is what the gods have made
As the best aid to mortal men in chasing troubles away.

This recommendation did not satisfy Menelaos, and he went on to visit his brother Agamemnon at Mycenae. The two brothers decided to send an embassy to Troy to demand the return of Helen. If the demand was not met, war would follow.

Priam, who was still king of Troy, received Agamemnon's embassy politely but rejected its chief demand. Paris would not give up Helen, and Priam would support his son. On the envoys' return Agamemnon and Menelaos had no choice but to fulfil their threat. Messengers were sent throughout Greece requiring fighting men to assemble for an expedition to Troy, led by the high king of Mycenae, to avenge the affront to his brother Menelaos. The expedition sailed eastwards across the Aegean, but – possibly because of distractions organized by Venus and Eros – landed on the coast of Asia much too close to Lesbos and a long way south of Troy. Unsure whether to proceed by land or sea, the Greeks set up a temporary camp in the lowlands of Teuthrania, the valley of the River Kaikos, but their landing was opposed by king Telephos and they were driven back to the sea. They returned to Greece ignominiously.

Now one of the mountain Nymphs of Ida had not been invited to join the wedding celebrations for Paris and Helen. Had she been invited, she would not have come. It was Oinone, Paris's former lover, who had now been left alone to bring up their son, Korythos, in the forest groves of Ida. Angry at his faithlessness, and fiercely jealous of Helen whom she blamed for seducing him, Oinone considered how it might be possible to break the attachment between the two. The first Greek expedition and its result became known in the fastnesses of Ida, and this gave Oinone her idea. She sent young Korythos to Greece with a single mission: to guide the Greeks to Troy. With Korythos as guide, and still under Agamemnon's leadership, the Greeks set out once more, from Aulis in Boiotia, and this time they encamped before the walls of Troy.

6

The Fall of Troy
and the Origin of Rome

THE GREEK SIEGE OF TROY LASTED TEN YEARS. IT WAS ENTIRELY CAUSED BY Helen's elopement with Paris, and this in turn was entirely caused by Venus's promise to Paris in return for her victory in the famous beauty competition. So it is no surprise to find that Venus was among those immortals who gave support to the Trojans. War was never Venus's concern, and the Trojan War will not be retold here as part of her biography. Yet she had caused the war, and she occasionally took an active part in it.

Paris, we remember, had rejected the bribe dangled in front of him by Athene. He was therefore inclined to lose his battles. He once unwisely found himself involved in single combat with Menelaos, a duel that might easily have concluded the war to nearly everybody's satisfaction – because with one of her husbands dead, nearly everybody, probably even Helen herself, would have been happy to see her claimed as legitimate spoils of victory by the other.

'If Paris kills Menelaos,' Agamemnon had proclaimed under the terms of truce, 'let him keep Helen and all her property, and we will go home in our ships. If red-haired Menelaos kills Paris, let the Trojans give back Helen and all her property, and pay such reparations as will be acceptable to us and impressive to those who come after us.'

Both sides had accepted Agamemnon's proclamation. Zeus, Helios and the other gods invoked by his libations had acceded to it. It was Venus, alone, who would not accept that her champion Paris should die fighting his rival for the very prize that she had already awarded to him. This was her first personal intervention on the battlefield of Troy.

Paris was not doing well. The lots had been cast and Paris had won the right to the first spearthrow. His accuracy was good, but his strength was inadequate. The spear struck Menelaos's shield and glanced off harmlessly. Now it was Menelaos's throw, and he was strong enough to send his spear straight through the leather of Paris's shield. Paris himself managed to escape injury, twisting away from the spearhead, but it had been a close thing. Next moment Menelaos was at him with his sword, which he brought crashing down on Paris's helmet. Luckily for Paris, the sword shattered; but Menelaos knew how to keep his advantage. He grabbed the helmet and dragged Paris bodily towards the watching line of Greek troops.

Venus never let her attention wander far from Troy and Mount Ida, where her champion Paris and her son Aeneas might at any time need her help. She was on the battlefield in a moment. Her first intervention was an unobtrusive one. She broke the chinstrap of Paris's helmet, an easy thing for a goddess to do, and he wriggled away free. Menelaos's momentary frustration can be imagined: this was a day when every piece of equipment he touched seemed to fail him. He turned and reached out for some other part of Paris – and then recoiled in utter astonishment. There was no one else on the duelling field. Venus's second intervention had been to gather Paris up in a cloud of mist, from which she deposited him in his bedroom, safe behind the walls of Troy.

Then she was off to find Helen. Disguising herself in the body of the old slave woman who had accompanied Helen from Sparta, Venus tugged at her robe. 'Come back to your own house, lady,' she said, 'your husband has fought well today and now he needs you. He looks as beautiful as ever – as if he were off to a dance, not back from the battlefield.'

But Helen looked into the face of her old servant and saw Venus's flashing eyes. As she penetrated the disguise Helen's heart stopped for a moment. She said:

'Lady, must you be his procuress?
Is Menelaos about to drag me home to Sparta in disgrace,
Has he beaten your beloved Paris in combat –
Is that why you are here with your lies?
Go to him yourself, if you like him so much.
Live apart from the gods, walk away from Olympos:
Then you can gaze at him and fawn around him
Till he makes you his woman, his slave!
No, I will not go to him and serve his bed.
It would be shameful. If I do, every woman in Troy
Will spit on me. I have enough heartache already.'

And Venus snapped:

'Don't try me too hard, slut, or I shall get angry.
I could hate you as much I have loved you till now.
I could abandon you to the hatred of both sides,
Trojans and Greeks. That would be an unpleasant death.'

Rebellious as she was, Helen knew she was in Venus's power. So she veiled her face, so that the women of Troy would not know her, and went to Paris, who lay all this time puzzling over his escape from Menelaos and trying not to recall how his opponent had had him on the run.

'You got away, then,' said Helen. 'Why don't you ever stand up to Menelaos? I want you either victorious or dead.'

'I'll beat him next time,' said Paris. 'Now come to bed. I want you, as much as I wanted you on the island of Kranae, that first night after we sailed from Sparta.' And so they lay together and made love, while Menelaos was still raging on the battlefield, quite unable to conceive what had become of the young Trojan who had stolen his wife and had thus far escaped his vengeance with Venus's help.

Not long afterwards Venus's own son, Aeneas, needed her help against the temporarily unstoppable Greek warrior Diomedes. Urged on by Athene, Diomedes knew that on this particular day every one of his opponents would be killed or forced into submission. His patron goddess had even warned him that he might meet immortals fighting for the Trojan cause. 'You must not attack gods or goddesses,' said Athene. 'There is one exception. You are quite safe in attacking Venus, should you happen to meet her.'

So when Aeneas and his friend Pandaros, in a chariot drawn by four magnificent stallions, sped towards Diomedes across the chaotic field of battle, Diomedes was ready for them. 'Do you see those horses?' he said to his companion Sthenelos. 'They are said to be of immortal race. Their grandsires were presented by Zeus to Tros as compensation for his young son Ganymede, whom Zeus had kidnapped and kept with him on Mount Olympos. It was a generous payment and Tros accepted it gladly. Anchises secretly allowed his own mares to be mounted by those immortal stallions, and these that now pull Aeneas's chariot are their descendants. They will soon be ours!'

No sooner had Pandaros reined in the horses than he was killed outright by Diomedes' spear. With the next thrust Aeneas was toppled from his chariot and rolled in the dust. He was unhurt, though shaken, and Venus was at once at hand to save her son's life. She enveloped him in her own robe and began to drag him away. Wrapped in this divine garment Aeneas could no longer be seen clearly by mortals; Venus, too, was invisible. But Diomedes was quite easily able to see where the robe was twisted and gripped in someone's invisible hand. Knowing the parentage of Aeneas he felt fairly sure that the interfering immortal must be Venus. To test his theory he stabbed at where her hand should be.

There was a piercing scream, and Aeneas was unceremoniously dropped. Fortunately Apollo (who, like Venus, favoured the Trojans) was at hand to take over the rescue of Venus's son. Diomedes got the horses.

Meanwhile Venus ran to the edge of the battlefield, where Ares was watching and attending to his own horses. The palm of her hand was dripping with ichor, the liquid that flows in the gods' veins, and the wound was stinging. 'Help me, brother!' she sobbed.

'I'd better drive you home,' said Ares, and in a few moments she was being comforted by her mysterious mother Dione.

'Which of the immortals did this to you, my child?' Dione asked. 'And why? Did they catch you doing something wicked?'

'It was no immortal,' Venus sobbed, her head on Dione's lap. 'It was Diomedes. Those Greeks are no longer content with fighting Trojans; now they are attacking us as well.'

'You are not the first immortal to be wounded by a human,' said her mother, wiping the darkening ichor from her skin. And with this soothing motion the wound was healed and the pain vanished.

Athene and Hera, who had never forgotten their defeat in the Judgement of Paris, observed this touching scene. 'Look, father Zeus,' said Athene, 'Venus's been up to her wicked tricks. I expect she was forcing some unlucky Greek girl into bed with a Trojan – she's always doing that – and she caught her poor little hand on the girl's brooch!'

Zeus smiled. 'Come here, Venus,' he said. 'This is something that you had promised to remember: the act of love is your province. Leave war to Ares and Athene.' Still, thanks to her intervention, Aeneas had escaped death at the hands of Diomedes.

There is only one subsequent occasion, in the course of the whole ten-year war, on which Venus overlooked her promise. Her mistake was forgivable, because this was the day on which rivalries among the Olympians rose to such a pitch that several of them took a direct hand in the fighting. Not surprisingly, it was Ares who started it by aiming his spear directly at the magic goatskin which Athene wore to protect her chest. Not even Zeus himself can penetrate this armour; certainly Ares could not. Athene sprang back out of his reach, picked up a massive boulder, and tossed it at Ares, hitting him squarely on the ear. He collapsed, temporarily stunned: his body covered seven acres, says the poet of the *Iliad*.

Once more Venus intervened to save a protégé of hers. She rushed on to the scene, knelt beside Ares and helped him to get up. The unlucky war god swayed to his feet and began to stumble away from the field of battle in the arms of his lover.

'Look, Athene,' said Hera, 'there's that bitch Venus on the battlefield again. Get her!'

Athene ran after the divine lovers. She needed no weapons for what she planned to do next: taking a wide swing she hit Venus full across the chest with the flat of her hand. Now it was Venus's turn to collapse in a heap, with Ares beside her. Athene stood over them in triumph. She said:

'I only wish all who fought for the Trojans were as invincible as Ares and as brave as Venus! In that case the war would have been over long ago.'

Venus merely smiled as she meditated the future of her son, his chosen band of Trojans, and their descendants.

The story of Helen, the *face that launched a thousand ships*, the cause of the eventual fall of Troy, was hard for many Greeks to come to terms with. Had she wanted to elope with Paris, or was she forced to do so by Venus and Eros? Was it true, as the poet of the *Iliad* thought, that by the tenth year of the war she despised Paris and the women of Troy despised her?

Could it perhaps be true that Helen never reached Troy at all? The Greek poet Stesichoros, after telling the Troy story in a way that was highly critical of Helen, was afflicted by blindness by Helen's supernatural power (or so his biographers said). After some years' reflection on the freedom of poets and the powers of offended goddesses, he wrote his famous *Palinode* to show that Helen was innocent. According to this revisionist narrative, Paris kidnapped Helen. Driven off course by storms, he landed in Egypt, where king Proteus rescued her from her abductor. But Hera, with whom defeat in the beauty competition still rankled, made a false Helen out of clouds, and Paris took this surrogate to Troy with him. Later, at the end of the ten-year siege, Menelaos returned home via Egypt as everyone knows. He, like Paris, was deceived by the false Helen, said Stesichoros; thinking that he had recaptured his wife, he was taking her home with him in triumph. In Egypt he found the real Helen still living. Having come to terms with his surprise, he persuaded king Theoklymenos, son of Proteus, to release her to him. In a twist to this theory – once started, historical revisionism never ends – it was sometimes said that Helen had never even boarded Paris's ship but that the god Hermes took her to Egypt out of harm's way. The real purpose of all this was to show that Helen, a nice Greek girl, was raped by Paris and escaped from him as soon as she could; or, much better still from a patriarchal point of view, she was never in his power at all. Admittedly it emerges from this revision of the Helen story that Menelaos, Paris, and all the Greek and Trojan warriors who fought on their behalf were fools and were fighting for nothing; but that, after all, is true of many wars.

In the real story, to which we now return, Helen was in Troy. There she heard news of the bitter fight in which Paris received a dangerous wound in the groin, and was carried from the battlefield to the secluded valley where the nymph Oinone still lived alone. He pleaded with her to forgive his desertion and cure him with her herbal skills. Oinone did not forgive so lightly, and Paris died.

Helen was now forced by king Priam to marry Paris's brother Deiphobos, and was ever more hated by the Trojans as the sole cause of the war. No end to her sadness was in sight; until, one night during the tenth year of the war, she caught the Greek warriors Odysseus and Diomedes in the act of emerging from a sewer which ran under the walls. They were disguised as beggars, and they had determined to enter Troy secretly with two aims: to steal the *Palladion*, the image of Athene whose presence preserved Troy from capture, and to make a reconnaissance in advance of their planned final assault on the city.

Faced with the decision whether or not to give them away, Helen knew what she must do. She helped them, led them to the *Palladion* and learned of the plan for the Wooden Horse; and thus she was ready to lead the women of Troy in Bacchanalian revelry when the Greek ships had apparently retreated and the mysterious Horse was dragged within the walls of Troy. Not only this, but while her hated husband, Deiphobos, lay sleeping she took away his sword. Menelaos and Odysseus, emerging from the Horse, broke into Deiphobos's house. They cut off his ears, nose and hands, and finally put him to death. Some said that Helen herself wielded the sword that killed Deiphobos.

Menelaos thus recaptured Helen as she lay, half-naked, in Deiphobos' bed, and once more he was immediately entranced by her beauty. He took her back to Sparta with him, and they lived together again as husband and wife. On this return journey they must have called at Rhodes, because in the temple of Athene at Lindos, in Roman times, you might have been shown a gold cup which had been dedicated there by Helen. Its distinctive shape was explained by the fact that the goldsmith had modelled it from her breast.

Most of the women and children of Troy were taken in captivity to Greece to live out their lives as slaves. Most of the men, those who had not already died in the fighting, were slaughtered.

For one group of Trojans, led by Venus's son Aeneas, a very different fate was reserved. He had been lucky to survive the ten-year war. Not only had Venus herself had to make him disappear from the battlefield on the day when he nearly fell to Diomedes; her good friend Poseidon had snatched Aeneas from danger on a different occasion, when he unwisely challenged the Greek hero Achilleus. Poseidon did not wish the line of Dardanos to be extinguished, and Venus had foretold to her lover Anchises that one day their son would rule the Trojans.

Some said that on the day of the Wooden Horse, when the Trojan seer Laokoon warned in vain of the danger with those famous words *'Beware the Greeks even when they bring gifts!'* Aeneas was among those who believed him, and immediately led a dissident party of Trojans out of the city to the relative safety of the hills of Ida. Others said that Aeneas was still in charge of Troy's defences till the moment of its fall, that same night, when the Greeks rushed out from their Horse and made him captive. They allowed him to choose one possession to take with him into slavery. Aeneas took on to his shoulders his father Anchises, crippled ever since the lightning strike. 'This is my only valued possession,' said Aeneas. The Greeks were so impressed by his filial piety that they allowed him and Anchises and Aeneas's young son Askanios to go free. But the Roman poet Vergil – who needed the hero of his *Aeneid* to see everything that happened on Troy's last day – has him wake up to find the Greeks already on the rampage. Helplessly he watches the capture of the palace, the killings of Priam and others, and the city's collapse into flames. Then he catches sight of Helen, who had taken refuge in a temple, and wonders whether to kill her in punishment for the destruction that she had brought on Troy (but this strange scene conflicts with the usual story, in which Helen was taken captive by Menelaos in Deiphobos's house; in any case Vergil had not completed the scene when he died and we do not know how he might have reconciled the two). As Aeneas meditates this decision he is accosted by his mother, the goddess of love, who reminds him of his duty to his father, wife and son, all three of whom she has so far managed to protect from the murderous Greeks.

'Do not blame the beauty of Spartan Helen, or the misbehaviour of Paris,' she continues: 'it is the anger of the gods that is turning Troy upside down.' With this, she lifts the veil cast over his mortal eyes by the darkness, mist and smoke, and shows him these gods at work: among them he sees the fearful Athene, astride the citadel, a dreadful light gleaming from the clouds that clothe her, tearing apart the masonry walls.

'Make your escape, my son,' the goddess of love tells him. 'I will be with you.'

With this dreadful vision of the city's fall still before his eyes, he finds his family and begins to lead a group of Trojans to safety on the mountain. In the chaos of their flight, however, he loses touch once more with his wife; she is killed at Troy.

The destiny of Aeneas (according to Vergil, his wife's ghost appeared to him in a vision and made this clear) was to voyage westwards and to lay the foundations of a new Troy in central Italy, far beyond the reach of Greek vengeance.

Some of Aeneas's story was told by Greeks. In the fourth century, Timaios, the great Greek historian of the west, claimed that Aeneas had negotiated safe conduct for his party of fleeing Trojans and had led them by land across northern Greece, finally reaching Bouthroton (which is now Butrint in Albania) where they took ship for Italy. Timaios picked up some or all of this from the early chronicler Hellanikos; the story goes back a long way.

In its full form, however, it is developed by Roman authors. It became their national history or founding myth, and it explains how Venus made herself the special patroness of Rome. This narrative will use the name Iulus for Aeneas's son, and Cupid for Venus's mischievous child, as do the Latin sources I am now following.

According to Vergil, after some years of indecisive wanderings, the Trojans, still led by Aeneas, were driven by a fierce storm to land on the North African coast. As the Trojans explored the neighbourhood of their landfall, they encountered a young hunting girl, with virgin face and virgin dress, carrying a bow and with a quiver of arrows at her back.

'You are not far from the newly founded city of Carthage,' she told them, 'a Phoenician colony ruled by queen Dido. Ask her for help and hospitality.'

As she turned away, a tint of rose glowed on her neck and an ambrosial scent wafted from her hair, and Aeneas realized, rather late in the day, that he had been speaking to his mother Venus once again.

Having encouraged Aeneas to visit Carthage, where he would certainly be invited to a welcoming banquet, Venus was halfway to completing her project to make Dido fall in love with him. All she had to do now was temporarily to substitute her own son, Cupid, for Aeneas's little son Iulus, whom Dido was due to meet at dinner.

'She will kiss and cuddle you, thinking you are Iulus,' she told Cupid, 'which puts you in an excellent position to breathe into her the fire of love and the poison of desire for Aeneas.'

Sure enough, Dido found herself ever more obsessed by this brave and resourceful warrior. They spent much time together. Eventually, while out hunting, they were surprised by a sudden storm, took shelter in a cave, and there, Vergil claims primly on Dido's behalf, they were 'married'. Earth, Fire and Air were their witnesses; Juno (the Greek Hera), goddess of marriage, gave the bride away. Or, rather, they made love, and the subsequent romance of Aeneas and Dido is another of the doomed affairs for which the love goddess must be blamed, for it ended in tragedy. Aeneas knew that he was destined to found his new Troy in Italy; he knew that the gods had not intended him and his Trojans to participate in the building of Carthage, as Dido hoped. The day came when he declared his intention to remain no longer, and on that day, as the Trojan ships sailed from Carthage northwards to their destined landfall, Dido mounted her own funeral pyre, sword in hand. Unable to face the loss of the man she loved, she stabbed herself to death.

Vergil's *Aeneid* tells this story as straight history, and a biographer of the love goddess is left to ask why she should set up a love affair that she knew to be hopeless and that led to Dido's suicide.

A clever biographer can find several answers. One answer is that this is not a traditional story: it is an invention by Vergil. But that won't do: the stories of the gods are all inventions by somebody, even if we seldom know by whom. In any case, Vergil really is building on an older story in which Aeneas fell in love with Dido's sister Anna: he merely makes the story more poignant by giving the starring role to the queen in person. A second answer is one that Vergil himself half-heartedly tries to put forward: the illicit lovemaking in the cave is really the fault of Juno, who caused the storm and deceitfully persuaded Venus that this would be a good idea. This won't do either: Venus alone had made Dido fall in love with Aeneas.

The third answer, the real answer, is that this is what the love goddess does. She causes desire, and with the willing help of her son she causes love. How rarely the two parties in a love affair share the same emotions, the same desires, the same hopes for the future! When such differences cause tragedy, those who believe in divine causation have, at least, someone to blame. Vergil's genius made the story of Dido and Aeneas far more universal, and far more painful, than the plot of the *Aeneid* – the founding myth of Rome – really required.

Aeneas's destiny was to found his new Troy at Alba Longa in Latium, not far from where Rome would one day rise. There, after many years of rule, he died, and Venus begged Jupiter, king of the gods, to allow her famous son to become an immortal. This request was not opposed by any of the gods, and Jupiter granted it. Venus herself attended to the necessary rites. She washed Aeneas's body in the River Numicius, which carried every mortal impurity down to the sea. When he was thus purified she perfumed him with spices and touched his lips with nectar and ambrosia. Thus her mortal son became a god, one to whom the

Romans offered sacrifice under the title *Indiges*. Iulus reigned at Alba Longa after him.

Centuries later his descendants Romulus and Remus would found the city of Rome, and through the centuries, as this city's power grew, its citizens regarded Venus as their protector.

She was the special patroness of the *gens Iulia*, the family to which Julius Caesar belonged. It was accepted that the family were descendants of Iulus, son of Aeneas, son of Anchises and Venus. Thus she was Caesar's direct ancestor across a gap of more than a thousand years, and it was said in Rome that when the knives were being sharpened for the conspiracy to assassinate Caesar in the Senate House on the Ides of March in 44 BC, Venus was at once aware of the threat to her offspring and demanded that the gods prevent it. She tried to protect him herself, it was said, by surrounding him with a March mist very much as she had protected Paris on the field of battle outside Troy. If it was so, this time she was unsuccessful.

'His fated lifespan is complete,' Jupiter said to her, 'but the achievements of his adopted son will be greater than his own, if that is possible. He will avenge his father in war, conquer Egypt, and found a monarchy that will survive for nearly fifteen hundred years.'

There was even an additional consolation for Venus. Caesar, like his distant ancestor Aeneas, became a god. The Romans had determined on this for themselves, but Jupiter signalled his consent unmistakeably. *On the first day of the Games given by his heir, Augustus, to mark his consecration,* so his biographer Suetonius wrote, *a long-haired star shone in the eastern sky from about an hour before sunset, and continued to do so for the following six days. It was believed that this was the soul of Caesar received into Heaven.*

7

The Goddess of Love

A COMET REALLY WAS SEEN AT THE TIME OF CAESAR'S DEATH — HALLEY'S comet, as we now call it — but it is easy to assume, since Suetonius uses the phrase *creditum est* 'it was believed', that he personally did not believe that the comet represented the soul of Caesar. It is easy to assume too, when Ovid details the conversation on Mount Olympus between Venus and Jupiter on whether Caesar's assassination should be permitted, that he does not believe in these gods at all. Those assumptions are *too* easy. Even the worldly wise authors who wrote under the early Roman empire did believe in their gods and goddesses — though 'truth' when writing about the gods was different from 'truth' when writing history.

In the *Art of Love*, a light-hearted poetic textbook of which the emperor Augustus strongly disapproved, Ovid writes that Venus is still to be found, in endless variety, in the great city whose foundations were laid by her son:

> As many wheatsheaves as are on Mount Gargaros,
>   as many grapes as on Lesbos,
> As many fish as in the sea, as many birds as are in the trees,
> As many stars as are in the sky, so many girls await you in Rome:
> Thus, in the city of Aeneas, his Mother is ever-present!

How is she present? Because the goddess Venus presides over sexual desire and the sexual act; because she makes it happen, and helps people

– and animals – to discover how it's done; because she is worshipped by women in love or looking for love, and by women who make men pay for sex; and because, for all these reasons, she symbolises and embodies sex. She does so even by virtue of her name, because *venus* means 'sex' in Latin; the word is linked with *vanas*, 'desire' in the earliest Sanskrit, *wunna*, 'joy' in the earliest German, and *wish* in English.

You pray to Venus to bring you success in love, and perhaps you will dare to ask her to curse the sexual attempts of one of your rivals. But Venus must not be offended. Better than anyone else she knows the pain of love, and will hit back if you mock her, making you suffer what she has suffered. She laughs at cowards, at those who hang back. She despises (according to Ovid) those who use aphrodisiacs: she will not allow her pleasures to be forced in such a way. As a writer you pray to her to help you find the words: so Ovid does, appropriately, at the opening of his *Art of Love*, the first two books of which, as he playfully claims, may serve as a textbook for Venus's son Cupid; in book three Ovid claims to have Venus's commission to teach the young women of Rome the rules and practices of love – including the details that might make them blush, because these details in particular are the work of Venus.

In a more serious mood, the philosophical poet Lucretius begins his great exposition of the world view of Epicurus with a prayer to Venus. He asks her to favour his enterprise because she is, quite simply, a life force of the universe; through her all creatures are conceived and come into existence. He also asks her – because the war god Mars himself sometimes sleeps in her arms, captivated by the incurable wound of love – to bring peace to Rome, riven by civil war. Lucretius can write all this and yet he can still argue, with Epicurus, that if there are gods at all they have no direct influence on affairs in this world of ours; he can do it because, whether or not there are gods, *venus* remains a life force of the universe, the one that tends to produce peace rather than war.

Her first temple in Rome, according to the historian Livy, was dedicated in 295 BC: if Livy is right, it is not clear for how long before that date Venus had been regarded by Romans as a goddess. In the course of the following century, at any rate, it became clear to Romans that their Venus was the same as the Aphrodite of the Greeks, and at a ceremony at which the Twelve Gods of Greece were propitiated with a banquet, when Rome was under attack from Hannibal in 217 BC, Venus shared a banqueting couch with Mars – whether as his 'sister', his lover or his wife, or because their spheres of influence were complementary, we are not told.

In one of her aspects, the Roman Venus was the goddess who owned the rocky peak of Eryx, on the north coast of Sicily. As such they called her Erycina, or Venus Erycina, and she was brought to Rome at the same date as that banquet for the Twelve Gods: her new temple in that year was dedicated by the city's most powerful magistrate, the dictator Q. Fabius Maximus Cunctator. Her great feast was the *Vinalia rustica*, on 19 August, and according to Ovid's poem *Fasti*, which catalogues the festivals of Rome, it was particularly observed by the prostitutes of the city: *Whores, celebrate the divinity of Venus! She is the best helper for a professional girl. Offer her incense. Ask in return for beauty and popularity; ask for charm, wit and repartee. Give to the Lady the watermint she loves, along with her own myrtle; give her garlands made of rushes, with roses interwoven.*

There was thus a long connection between the goddess Erycina and the city of Rome. Roman magistrates, officials and businessmen on tour in Sicily would make a point of visiting Eryx and enjoying the opportunities for pleasure offered by this famous sanctuary, which was perhaps the most westerly of the many centres of sacred prostitution over which the goddess of love presided. Women who worked there often began their careers as 'slaves of the goddess', but were able to make savings, buy their freedom, and perhaps eventually run a business in or around the temple. Evidently several languages were spoken at Eryx. The Romans naturally identified the local goddess with Venus, and the Greeks with Aphrodite, but both knew that her real name was *Erykine* and that the origin of the sanctuary was as a native Sicilian place of worship. Its first foreign visitors – long before the Romans became involved with it – were probably Carthaginians. Greeks said that king Eryx, its founder, was the son of Aphrodite and of the mortal Boutes, one of the Argonauts; they also said that after sailing from Carthage, Aeneas, the better-known son of the love goddess, had paused at Eryx to make offerings at the famous shrine.

The Greek goddess Aphrodite is known from the earliest literature. Like Venus, she represents the force of the earth's fertility; she creates desire among humans, she makes gods desire mortals, and it is also the work of Aphrodite to make the grass and the flowers grow, which is why flowers sprang up under her feet as she first stepped ashore on Cyprus. She is called *golden Aphrodite* and *the foam-born (aphrogenea)* and *the laughter-loving*.

The stories involving Aphrodite tell of the power of sexual desire, the impossibility of shutting it out, and the need for men and women to make their peace with the love goddess. She was angry with those who denied her divinity or refused to worship her, such as Hippolytos in Euripides's tragedy; such people came to a bad end. She favoured those who offered her special honour, notably Theseus, the sexually liberated national hero of Athens. She gave beauty to women and desirability to men. Like other gods, she sometimes travelled the Earth in disguise. To the ferryman Phaon, it was said, she appeared as a poor old woman who had no money for her fare. He carried her anyway, and was rewarded with – what? Youthful beauty? An unguent that made him irresistible to women? One night with Aphrodite? All three versions exist.

There were venerable images of Aphrodite in armour; however, by contrast with most other goddesses, it was traditional in classical Greek religious iconography to depict her nude, or in the act of undressing, or at any rate aware of her body, perhaps concealing her sexual parts in a way that at the same time drew attention to them. Special worship was offered to her under the title *Aphrodite kallipyge*, 'Aphrodite with the nice ass'. Ancient statues have been recovered that scholars confidently identify with this aspect of the goddess. On the promontory at Knidos, one of the Greek cities on the Aegean coast of Asia Minor, the temple of Aphrodite had an unusual design, open on four sides so that mariners passing the headland were able to view from all angles the magnificent nude 'Aphrodite of Knidos', one of the most famous works of the classical sculptor Praxiteles.

You prayed to Aphrodite for beauty and success in love. Perhaps you wished to make one particular conquest. This is the desire expressed by Sappho, poetess of Lesbos, in the poem that stood first in her collected works – one of the few poems of hers that now survives complete:

Splendidly enthroned immortal Aphrodite, cunning child of Zeus,
I beg you –
do not tear my heart, lady, with sick fears and horrors –
come to me now,
if ever you listened to my cry from very far away, and left your
father's house and harnessed your golden chariot to its pair of
fine strong sparrows whose swift wings sped you from Heaven
through the middle air down to the black earth and suddenly
you were there, goddess, and you asked me, with a smile on your
immortal face,
'Did you call me? Does it hurt? What is it that you want so much,
wild heart? Whom shall I make to be your beloved? Who has
spurned you, Sappho?
'One who runs from you will soon run after you; one who will not
accept your gifts, will soon give; one who does not love you will
soon love you even if she does not want to!'
So come to me just once more;
ease the pain: this that my heart wants to make happen, make it
happen; fight on my side.

Perhaps you wished for success in general, like the woman of the third century AD who performed a magic rite, said a magic word and spoke thus:

'Kypris, come to me every day of my life … grant me now victory, reputation and beauty before all men and women.'

There were many such spells, general and specific. Some meant no harm to anyone, as when Ladike, the Greek lady of Kyrene who married king Amasis of Egypt, prayed successfully to Aphrodite (so it was said) to cure her husband's impotence. Other spells would bind a person to a lover even if unwilling, or make a husband impotent with partners other than his wife. Magical practices were often needed to make these prayers and spells work. The strangest was the use of the *iynx*, the bird called wryneck in English, which must be caught and fastened live to a wheel which was turned while the spell was recited; but this became too complicated, and model wrynecks were made. It was said that Kleopatra, the famously seductive queen of Egypt, used the magic of the *iynx* to bind three Romans to her successively, Caesar, Mark Antony and Augustus. It did not work in the last case.

At the crossroads of Greece was the city of Corinth, and on the massively mountainous citadel of Corinth was the city's most honoured temple, that of Aphrodite. *Aphrodite Pandemos* was worshipped in many cities – 'public Aphrodite', the special patroness of courtesans and prostitutes – but Corinth was truly the centre of sacred prostitution in Greece. When the city offered prayers at a time of crisis, the prostitutes, the slaves of the goddess, were invited to take part in the procession and sacrifice; this occurred notably when the Persian invaders threatened Greece in 480 BC, and it is a matter of record that they did not capture Corinth or penetrate beyond. Not many years afterwards the poet Pindar addressed the courtesans of Corinth in an ode that now survives in fragments:

> *Young girls who welcome many strangers,*
> *Handmaids of Persuasion in rich Corinth,*
> *Who burn the yellow tears of the green incense tree*
> *As often as you fly in your thoughts to heavenly Aphrodite,*
> *   mother of the Erotes:*
> *She has privileged you, children, far above all reproach,*
> *To pick the ripe fruits of youth in your beds of desire.*
> *When Need compels, all is beautiful …*

One way in which the number of slaves of the love goddess tended to increase was that individuals who made a prayer to her would often vow to dedicate girls to her service if the prayer was answered; the sports personality Xenophon of Corinth, for example, dedicated a hundred slave girls to Aphrodite in gratitude for his athletic victory at Olympia in 464 BC, a victory that Pindar himself was commissioned to celebrate.

Aphrodite is also called *Kythereia*, the lady of Kythera. Her biography supplies no very good reason for this. The ancient traveller Pausanias says that on Kythera there was a temple of *Ourania*, 'the Heavenly goddess', which was the oldest sanctuary of Aphrodite in the whole of Greece, with an archaic wooden image of the goddess wearing armour. But since there were so many sanctuaries of Aphrodite, why did all Greece associate her with Kythera? This island, off the southern coast of the Peloponnese, was a trading place in very early times: Egyptians were familiar with Kythera in the mid third millennium BC and Levantines by the early second; soon after that the Minoans of Crete had established a settlement on Kythera. The Mycenaean kings of Pylos recorded 'slave women from Kythera', duties unspecified, in their palace inventories in the fourteenth century BC. Perhaps the goddess of love was once worshipped in many languages on Kythera, which perhaps was long ago a centre of prostitution as well as of trade; perhaps Aphrodite spread her worship northwards into Greece from the island known to the earliest epic poets as *sacred Kythera*: but such guesses have at present little evidence to back them.

Greek poets call Aphrodite *Kypris* more often than they use any of her other names. In her Greek biography Cyprus is where she came ashore or was 'born', but that is not the only reason for the name. Greeks also spoke specifically of her sanctuary at Paphos, close to the southern coast of the island, and Roman poets often called her *Paphia* for this reason.

Paphos was an important place, linked by trade and diplomacy with Mycenaeans and later Greeks to the west, with Egypt to the south, and with Phoenicia and Assyria to the east. The ancient shrine of the love goddess contained a white statue, not in human form but in conical shape – an abstract image that was often depicted on coins and apparently still survives, for just such an object was found among the ruins of a big Roman temple of the love goddess. Once a year the people of Paphos assembled, men and women together, to go in procession from the new city of Paphos on the coast to the old city, a mile inland, and the ancient shrine. Its real fame was as an oracle, at which the worshipper made a sacrifice of his or her choice. Titus, the future Roman emperor, stopped at Paphos on his way to Palestine to fight alongside his father, Vespasian, in AD 69, and was assured by the priest – a direct descendant of the legendary king Kinyras – of success in his campaigns.

On the mainland to the north of Cyprus – in Anatolia, or Turkey as we know it now – there was no widely known deity to be identified with the Greek and Roman love goddess. There were several important centres of sacred prostitution, but in general it was the Mother of the Gods who presided over them.

To the south lies Egypt, among whose gods and goddesses Isis bears the closest resemblance to Venus, while Osiris may be likened to Adonis: they were not normally identified, however, and in fact in later Greece and Italy Isis was widely worshipped under her own name.

To the east we enter the territory of Astarte (as she was sometimes called in Greek), the same love goddess who was Ashtaroth (in Aramaic) and Ishtar (in Akkadian, the documentary language of Assyria and Babylon); the makers of Akkadian epics and hymns drew many of their ideas from the Sumerian literature of early southern Mesopotamia, identifying their own Ishtar with the goddess who in the very different Sumerian language was called Inanna. Ishtar was the daughter of the sky god An, goddess of the storehouse, Lady of the Date Clusters. Inanna was the Queen of Heaven, the daughter of the Moon and brother of the Sun, the Morning and Evening Star, and 'the goddess who loves apples and pomegranates'. The New Year celebrations of ancient Sumer culminated in the ritual marriage of the reigning monarch to Inanna, a marriage that ensured for the coming year the fertility of humans, animals and plants. Erech, the Mesopotamian city that was the focus of the cult of Ishtar, was a centre of sacred prostitution. Ishtar and Inanna, like Aphrodite and Venus, acknowledged the prayers and responded to the magic practices of women who hoped by this means to make themselves beautiful, to be desired by all, or to be loved faithfully by one person to the exclusion of all others.

The four centuries that followed the assassination of Julius Caesar marked the spread across the Roman empire and the Near East of monotheism – the belief that there is only one god. Except in unusual places like Palestine, previously it was only self-conscious intellectuals who had spoken of 'the divine' or 'the god' with the implication that divinity need not be divided into many individuals with different characters and histories. But Judaism was migrating through the region and Christianity was spreading widely – at first particularly among slaves and the poor, but eventually among all social groups. By the fourth and fifth centuries those who still worshipped the ancient gods were on the defensive.

The 'pagan', pre-Christian religions of Europe and the Near East had room for several different approaches to worship. Many people regarded themselves as devotees of one single god selected from the ancient pantheon, and had given only perfunctory respect to others. This attitude could move into monotheism without difficulty, especially if the favoured deity was male, such as Mercury or Mithras. But for Aphrodite, Venus, Astarte and their analogues the spread of monotheism brought an inexorable decline. Among their most faithful and single-minded devotees had been prostitutes, many of whom, down to the period of Caesar and Augustus and for some time after, were still technically slaves of the love goddess, living in her great temple precincts in Sicily, Greece, Anatolia and the East. Temple prostitution gradually gave way to commercial prostitution in the increasingly urban empire, and each year more and more of the workers in this industry were Christians. Although in those early centuries there were certainly many unexpected hybrid forms of belief, being fully Christian eventually meant that one could not also be a worshipper of the love goddess, or of any goddess.

Another approach was to honour a god or goddess whose speciality was appropriate to an occasion or to a landmark in life. Thus the love goddess had been especially worshipped by girls and young women, about to be married and newly married. This worship did not suddenly cease either, and in some works of art made for Christians, in the last years of the empire, Aphrodite or Venus can still be seen presiding over the toilette of a bride, sometimes assisted by her winged son. Eventually she disappears here also: she will have been supplanted, sometimes, by temporary or permanent devotion to the Virgin Mary.

During the Middle Ages the love goddess was hidden, except for occasional appearances in illuminated manuscripts of classical authors such as Vergil and Ovid.

At the Renaissance she reappeared, though not as an object of worship. Now that the competition between paganism and Christianity was over, those who read the ancient texts with fresh eyes were able to develop the idea of gods as symbols, an idea that really is present in the texts. Thus Aphrodite or Venus becomes a symbol of sexual desire in general and of the sexual act, and Cupid or Eros becomes a symbol of 'falling in love' and of the sexual love that is felt for one person.

When artists of modern times depict Venus, their aims and assumptions are rather different from those of ancient sculptors and painters. They are not making an image representing the artist's own devotion, nor one to which worship will be offered by others, nor one before which incense will be burned – in Europe those roles are now reserved for Christian icons. They are as aware as ever of the 'biography' of Venus as retold in this book, and the image that they create often narrates an incident of her life; but it comes from their classical reading and not from oral tradition, to which ancient artists were often responding. But, finally, ancient painters and sculptors used all their skill and devotion to depict ideal female beauty in the body of Venus, the goddess of sexual desire; and their modern counterparts still do the same, because Venus, though to them she is only historically a goddess, is still as much as ever the symbol of sexual desire.

Writers, too, can use the same stories that their ancient counterparts used, and can play with styles and genres to similar effect. To begin with some ancient examples, the story of Cupid and Psyche, as told by Apuleius, has the atmosphere of folk tale. The story of Ares and Aphrodite, as told in the *Odyssey*, could be the subject of a humorous short epic for a late evening audience. The story of the birth of Venus, as told by Hesiod, is a cosmogonic episode, true with the truth of mysticism. Turning to modern examples, Shakespeare in *Venus and Adonis* (like Ovid in the *Metamorphoses*) is exploring the successes and catastrophes of human emotional entanglements; the choice of mythical characters in a fantasy setting leaves these authors as free as ever to explore the extremes. As told in seventeenth-century French burlesque verse by Coypeau d'Assoucy, the story of *Le Jugement de Paris* aims to amuse an urbane coterie of readers, classically educated, Christian but not much troubled by any religion; Lucian, who had told the same story in the second century as a comic dialogue, has a similar readership in mind, 'pagan' and without illusions.

Caesar was visible in the night sky only for a few days immediately after his apotheosis; but Venus is still to be seen there.

The brightest of all the 'wandering stars' or planets was thought by the earliest Greeks to be two different objects: the morning star, *Phosphoros* or *Heosphoros*, which is often seen in the east in the hour before sunrise to announce the coming of the Sun; and the evening star, *Hesperos*, often seen in the west soon after the Sun has gone down.

Both the Sumerians and the Egyptians, observing that the two appeared alternately on a regular cycle, had correctly deduced long ago that they were in fact a single object. The first Greek who became aware of this fact was apparently the mysterious philosopher and mathematician Pythagoras, who had travelled in the East and was said to have learned the Egyptian language. The Romans learned their astronomy from the Greeks, and accepted this fact without further question.

We still use the Roman name for the planet which had once been thought of as morning star and evening star, the planet we now know to be the second in the solar system. This name was *Venus*, the name of their love goddess. The Romans called it this because Pythagoras, or some other Greek in his time, had used the name of *Aphrodite's star* for the planet, and this name had become established among Greek scientists. The Greek name was not chosen at random. Although they had a different name for the planet, the Babylonians considered Ishtar to be its patroness; they borrowed this idea from the Sumerians, for whom *Inanna* was the name both of the love goddess and of the brightest planet. Pythagoras or a contemporary, while imbibing the astronomical knowledge of the Near East, learned of this link and adopted it into Greek.

So the association between the love goddess and the planet Venus is at least 4700 years old. Of all the ways in which she is commemorated, this is the simplest and the most enduring.

Life Notes

THE GODS ARE AGELESS AND IMMORTAL. THEY CAN BE INJURED, BUT THEY cannot easily be killed. There are twelve gods of Mount Olympos, listed below. There are also many other gods, and some of them are much older than these twelve.

The gods travel easily between Earth and Mount Olympos, and they often spend time on Earth in human disguise, but the journey to the Underworld is as difficult and fearsome for them as it is for humans.

Nymphs, Satyrs and other spirits of the wild places of Earth and Ocean are ageless but not immortal. If threatened by death or rape they may, with a god's help, be transformed into an animal or tree. Thus they escape the threat; but the transformation is permanent.

Mortals are subject to disease, old age and death. Seventy years is the usual span of their brief lives. In ancient times they used to live longer, some say.

Occasionally goddesses take mortal men as their lovers. Such a man is almost certain to be punished, later in life, with some permanent paralysis or sickness. However, the child of the love affair benefits from a double inheritance. He or she is likely to play a unique role in human history, and may, eventually, become immortal. Two examples are Aeneas, son of Venus and Anchises; and Achilleus, temperamental hero of the Greek siege of Troy, who was son of the Nereid Thetis and the mortal king Peleus.

Here are the Greek and *Latin* names of the twelve Olympian gods. Zeus, *Jupiter* or *Jove* is their ruler. He is the twin brother of Hera, *Juno*; their brother is Poseidon, *Neptunus*; their sister is Demeter, *Ceres*. The rest of the twelve Olympians, as usually listed, are Athene, *Minerva*; Aphrodite, *Venus*; Ares, *Mars*; Hephaistos, *Vulcanus*; Apollo; Artemis, *Diana*; Hermes, *Mercurius*; Hestia, *Vesta*.

The Underworld is the kingdom of Hades, *Pluto*. He seized the virgin daughter of Demeter to be his consort. She is called *Proserpina* in Latin and sometimes Persephone in Greek, but many Greek writers avoid naming her: they call her *kore*, 'the Maiden'.

Among the gods who began their life as mortals, and came to Olympos after the rest, are Dionysos, *Bacchus*; Herakles, *Hercules*; Asklepios, *Aesculapius*. Aineias, *Aeneas*, the child of Venus and Anchises, is one among several founders of cities who were worshipped as gods. The list is not closed. Julius Caesar, distant descendant of Aeneas, was the first Roman of later times to be worshipped as a god after his death. The same honour was accorded to Caesar's adopted son Augustus and to several later emperors.

Zeus, Hera, Poseidon and Demeter were the children of Kronos or *Saturnus* (whom Zeus displaced as king of the gods) and his sister Rhea. Kronos had himself supplanted his father Ouranos, *Uranus*. At the beginning of all things Ouranos 'the Sky', who lay above, rained upon Gaia 'the earth' who lay below, and that primeval act of intercourse is how gods, mortals and all the living things in the world were created. The Titans were among the children of Ouranos and Gaia; they eventually fought the Olympian gods and were defeated. Gaia is also said to have mated with Pontos, the 'Deep Sea'; Nereus, an ancient marine god, was their child.

Helios the Sun, Selene the Moon, and Eos the Dawn, are siblings. They are children of the Titan Hyperion. Among other 'non-Olympian' gods are the Kabeiroi, who belong to the island of Samothrake and preside over mystery rites there. Also in this category is Seilenos, a very ancient god of Earth, attendant of Dionysos and father or grandfather of the Satyrs. Adonis, one of the lovers of Venus, is a god without any Olympian ancestry; Greeks borrowed him from the Near East, where his best-known name was Tammuz. The sea-goddess Thetis is the leader of the fifty Nereids, who are daughters of the nymph Doris and of Nereus.

The strange and disputed parentage of Venus is discussed in chapter one. Dione, a sea-goddess and possibly a Titan, is often said to be her mother; Zeus is occasionally said to be her father. The ambiguity is a hint that Venus–Aphrodite, like Adonis, was in the distant past a migrant goddess; she was a newcomer to Mount Olympos. Hephaistos, her husband, and Ares, her first lover, were both Olympian gods and were among the offspring of Zeus and Hera.

Here are the children of Venus. Poseidon was the father of Herophilos and Rhodos. Phobos, Deimos and Harmonia are her offspring by Ares. The physically bisexual Hermaphroditos, *Hermaphroditus*, is her son by Hermes. Her child by Dionysos is Priapos, *Priapus*. As to Peitho and the mischievous Eros (*Cupido*, *Amor*), Aphrodite is generally said to have been their mother, but there is no agreement on the identity of their father.

The founder of Troy was generally said to be Dardanos, son of Zeus by the star Elektra, one of the seven Pleiades. Dardanos's son was Erichthonios, whose son was Tros. Ganymedes, younger son of Tros, became immortal when he was taken from the slopes of Mount Ida by Zeus to be his boy lover and cupbearer. Tros was succeeded as ruler of Troy by his elder son, Ilos, whose son was Laomedon, whose son was Priam. Priam's many children included Paris, whose seizure of Helen was the immediate cause of the Trojan War; Hektor, who was the hero of the Trojan defence; Kreousa (see below); and Kassandra, the prophetess who became Agamemnon's captive.

In the course of one of his many sexual adventures, it is said, Zeus once adopted temporarily the shape of a swan. The unwilling object of his love, briefly deceived by the disguise, was either the goddess Nemesis or a mortal woman named Leda, wife of king Tyndareos of Sparta. The egg that resulted from this mating was, at all events, hatched by Leda. Her children – variously described as offspring of Zeus or of Tyndareos – were the twin heroes and gods, Kastor (*Castor*) and Polydeukes (*Pollux*), and two mortal women. These two are Helen, who married Menelaos and was abducted by Paris; and Klytaimestra (*Clytemnestra*), who married Menelaos's brother Agamemnon, king of Mycenae. Klytaimestra murdered Agamemnon and Kassandra when the Greeks returned from Troy.

Anchises was a grandson either of Ilos or of Laomedon. By Venus he had a famous son, Aineias (*Aeneas*), and (some said) a less famous second son, Lyros. Aeneas married Kreousa (*Creusa*), a daughter of Priam; she died on the night when Troy fell. His son was Askanios (*Iulus*), said to be the ancestor of the *gens Iulia*. The most famous member of this Roman family was Gaius Julius Caesar.

Throughout this book I use *Venus* as the name of the classical love goddess. I do this because, ever since classical times, *Venus* has been a more familiar name in literature and art than the Greek equivalent, Aphrodite; it remains more familiar in modern English. I call her son *Aeneas*, using this Latin form of his name in place of the Greek Aineias, because he is a minor figure in Greek legend but the hero of the founding myth of Rome.

Apart from these two special cases, I use the forms of names appropriate to the origin of the myths and legends retold in this book. Since most of the stories are Greek, Greek names appear most often.

Greek and English use different alphabets. There are various ways of converting between the two, and that is why Greek names have many different spellings in English. In this book the spellings are intended to be close to the Greek original. In some other books, especially in classic English literature, you will find Latin forms of Greek names (including

-ae- for -ai-, -u- for -ou-, -us for -os, -a for -e, -i or -oe for -oi). In books published in Greece you find forms reflecting modern Greek pronunciation (*Kriti* for Crete, *Omiros* for Homer). The variations in English spelling tell one nothing about the form of the original Greek name; one simply learns to ignore them.

The following forms of Greek names used in this book are not Greek but traditional English: Athens (Greek *Athenai*), Thebes (*Thebai*), Corinth (*Korinthos*), Sparta (*Lakedaimon* or *Sparte*), Troy (*Ilion, Troia*), Thrace (*Thrake*), Rhodes (*Rhodos*), Crete (*Krete*), Centaur (*Kentauros*), Satyr (*Satyros*), Mainad (*Mainas*), Ocean (*Okeanos*), Ganymede (*Ganymedes*), Helen (*Helene*), Priam (*Priamos*), Homer (*Homeros*), Odyssey (*Odysseis*), Iliad (*Ilias*), Hesiod (*Hesiodos*), Pindar (*Pindaros*), Aristotle (*Aristoteles*), Plato (*Platon*), Plutarch (*Ploutarchos*). The following Greek names are used here in their Latin form: Cerberus (Greek *Kerberos*), Taenarum (*Tainaron, Tainaros*), Phoenicia (*Phoinike*), Ida (*Ide*), Mycenae (*Mykene, Mykenai*), Scythia (*Skythia*), Caria (*Karia*).

The following forms of Latin names used here are not Latin but traditional English: Ovid (Latin *Ovidius*), Vergil (*Vergilius*), Cupid (*Cupido, Amor*, Greek *Eros*), Lucian (*Lucianus*, Greek *Loukianos*), Rome (Latin *Roma*).

Sources

THE MOST ANCIENT GREEK SOURCE FOR THE APHRODITE STORY WAS THE *Kypria*, an epic poem probably of the sixth century BC – thus not much later in origin than the *Iliad* and *Odyssey* attributed to Homer. It narrated the antecedents and early years of the Trojan War, beginning, perhaps, with the Judgement of Paris. The *Kypria* is lost, but I have quoted some surviving fragments from it in the text. Outlines of its contents are given by Apollodoros, *Library* (see below) and by the Byzantine author Photios, whose *Library* includes a summary of a lost work by Proklos outlining all the early Greek epics: for this and other surviving evidence for the *Kypria* see West 2003.

Not much later than the *Kypria* is the *Homeric Hymn to Aphrodite*, an early Greek narrative poem (not composed by Homer, in spite of its traditional title) written in praise of the goddess and telling the story of her love affair with Anchises.

The two major Roman sources for Venus and her adventures are also epic poems, by Vergil and Ovid respectively. Both were written at the time of the emperor Augustus (30 BC – AD 14). These are literary epics; in using traditional tales – as they do, most of the time – these authors control the selection, form and message in a far more personal and planned way than the early Greek poets who drew on an oral tradition. Ovid's *Metamorphoses* is a collection of myths and legends of Greek origin that involve transformations (such as that of Smyrna into a myrrh tree). Ovid concludes with a brief outline of the Aeneas story, but the classic narrative of Aeneas had been written, not many years before, by

Vergil. His *Aeneid* reworked the earlier Greek versions of the adventures of Aeneas after the fall of Troy.

Apuleius's fantastic Latin narrative *Metamorphoses* includes the famous myth or fairy tale of Cupid and Psyche; it appears as a story within the main story of Lucius, the man who was turned into a donkey. One of Lucian's satirical Greek *Dialogues of the Gods* is an amusing sketch of the Judgement of Paris, and another relates the trapping of Ares and Aphrodite by Hephaistos. Apuleius and Lucian both lived in the second century AD.

Finally, the *Library* of Apollodoros, written at an unknown date probably under the Roman empire, is a careful, unsmiling summary of Greek mythology. The edition by J. G. Frazer is useful both for its English translation and for its very detailed notes on additional sources for each story.

The stories of Inanna and Ishtar are to be found gathered in several sources in English translation. One standard collection is *Ancient Near Eastern texts relating to the Old Testament*, edited by J. B. Pritchard. There is also a useful collection entitled *Myths from Mesopotamia* by Stephanie Dalley; finally there is a collection of texts about Inanna, in free and often conjectural translations, by Diane Wolkstein and S. N. Kramer.

Shakespeare's poem *Venus and Adonis* (1593) is available in many editions. The *Jugement de Paris* by Charles Coypeau d'Assoucy (1648) can be found on the Web at the site gallica.bnf.fr maintained by the Bibliothèque Nationale.

For full details of the translations mentioned in this section see 'Further Reading', pp. 149–51.

Chapter 1: The Birth of Venus

The emergence of Aphrodite from the sea is the opening scene in the *Homeric Hymn to Aphrodite*. Many centuries later the story was told as an aside in the long epic of Dionysos by Nonnos (*Dionysiaka* 13.432-463). On Dione and her origin see Hesiod, *Theogony* 353; Apollodoros, *Library* 1.1.3, 1.2.7. On Aphrodite's male ancestry see *Iliad* 3.374 and elsewhere; *Odyssey* 8.308, 320 (part of a story ascribed to the fictional Demodokos); Epimenides 3 B 19 Diels and Kranz. The story of the castration of Ouranos and its consequences is told by Hesiod, *Theogony* 154-206.

The myth of Inanna and Enkil is usually known as 'Inanna and the God of Wisdom': see Wolkstein and Kramer 1983 pp. 4-20.

On Aphrodite's *kestos himas* or embroidered band see *Iliad* 14.214-217 (with the commentary by Janko 1992); *Kyranides* 1.10.49-69 (translation and comment in Faraone 1999). For the Hours and the adorning of Aphrodite see *Homeric Hymns* 6 (the shorter *Homeric Hymn to Aphrodite*).

Chapter 2: Marriage and Adultery

On the throwing of Hephaistos down from Olympos see *Homeric Hymn to Apollo* 316-321; *Iliad* 18.395-405, 1.590-594. The philosopher Plato (*Republic* 378d) had heard this story, but he also knew a quite different one, that Hephaistos as a boy or young man had tried to intervene to protect his mother Hera when Zeus was beating her; Zeus had angrily thrown him out of Olympos, and thus he became lame. Plato heartily disapproved of both versions because they depicted the gods as childish, cruel and generally no better than humans; in the *Republic* he made Sokrates argue that such tales should not be told to children.

The story of the trick throne is mentioned by Alkaios fragment 349 Lobel and Page; Pindar fragment 283 Snell and Maehler; Pausanias 1.20.3; Hyginus, *Fables* 166. The triumphant procession in which Dionysos and the Satyrs bring Hephaistos to Mount Olympos is a favourite subject with ancient and modern painters. The episode was depicted on stage by Epicharmos in *Hephaistos or the Serenaders*, but this play does not survive. It is mentioned by Pausanias 3.17.3; pseudo-Libanios, *Narratives* 30.1 Westermann.

The famous story of the trapping of Ares and Aphrodite is told by the fictional poet Demodokos in *Odyssey* 8.266-369. Many centuries later the Roman poet Ovid tells it again, twice, in *Art of Love* 2.561-592 and in *Metamorphoses* 4.167-189, but without adding anything to the

Odyssey version. The scene is depicted in a sketch by the Greek satirical author Lucian (*Dialogues of the Gods* 17).

On the various relationships of Hephaistos and Aphrodite see *Iliad* 5.355-363, 18.382-383, 21.391-433; Hesiod, *Theogony* 945-946; *Homeric Hymn to Apollo* 182-206; Pausanias, *Guide to Greece* 3.17.5, 5.18.5. Aphrodite is described in the *Iliad* as daughter of Zeus and Dione, which does in fact make her Ares's half-sister; on the other hand lovers and spouses might address one another as 'brother' and 'sister'. For the children of Ares and Aphrodite see *Iliad* 4.439-440, 15.119-120; *Shield of Herakles* 463-466. Semele's child was Dionysos, who was thus the great-grandson of Aphrodite. How then could Dionysos be involved in the bringing of Hephaistos to Mount Olympos, before Aphrodite had even married him? There are many anachronisms in Greek mythological stories, but this one may show that there is something dubious about the famous story of Aphrodite's marriage to Hephaistos and unfaithfulness to him.

Many sources hint at the punishment of Eos and her subsequent love affairs (Apollodoros, *Library* 1.4.4-1.4.5 and 3.14.3; see Frazer's footnotes), naming Kleitos (*Odyssey* 15.249-251), Kephalos (Hesiod, *Theogony* 986-987; Euripides, *Hippolytos* 454; Pausanias 3.18.12; Antoninus Liberalis, *Metamorphoses* 41; their son was Phaethon according to Hesiod, *Theogony* 987); Orion (as narrated by Kalypso in *Odyssey* 5.121-124; see also scholia on this passage).

Chapter 3: The Children of Aphrodite

On the offspring of Poseidon and Aphrodite see Pindar, *Olympian Odes* 7.14 and 8.24 with scholia. The Kolossos of Rhodes stood at the harbour mouth of Rhodes Town. The many sources that mention the parentage of Erichthonios include Apollodoros, *Library* 3.14.6; see Frazer's footnote. His name seems to mean 'wool + earth' in Greek: it looks as though the story was invented to explain the name.

The two versions of the story of Hermaphroditos are told by Diodoros of Sicily 4.6.5 and by Ovid, *Metamorphoses* 4.285-388. For Priapos the sources include Diodoros of Sicily 4.6.1; Pausanias 9.31.2;

Scholia on Apollonios of Rhodes 1.932; Lucian, *Dialogues of the Gods* 23; Petronius, *Satyrica*; and the collection of anonymous Latin poems called *Priapea*.

On Peitho see Sappho fragment 200 Lobel and Page; Pindar fragment 107 Bowra [Athenaeus 574a]; Hermesianax 11. For Zelos and Apate see *Orphica* fragment 127; Apate was a daughter of *Nyx* 'Night' according to Hesiod, *Theogony* 224.

Many sources hint at the parentage of Eros (Cicero, *On the Nature of the Gods* 3.23; *Ciris* 134), naming Zephyros and Iris (Alkaios fragment 327 Lobel and Page [Plutarch, *Amatorius* 20]); Erebos and Nyx or Aither and Nyx (Akousilaos 2 F 6); Eileithyia (Pausanias 9.27.2 citing Olen); Gaia and Ouranos (Sappho fragment 198 Lobel and Page); Aphrodite (Bakchylides 8.73; Aischylos, *Suppliants* 1043); Aphrodite and Ouranos (Sappho fragment 198 Lobel and Page); Aphrodite and Ares (Simonides fragment 575 *PMG*). See also Hesiod, *Theogony* 119-122; Plato, *Symposium* 178b; Aristotle, *Metaphysics* 1.4; *Orphic Hymns* 5; Meleagros, *Epigrams* 50. For the weapons of Eros see Euripides, *Medeia* 530-531, *Iphigeneia at Aulis* 543-551, *Hippolytos* 38, 141-147, 236-238, 1303. Persuasion similarly uses a whip when Medeia is to be made to fall in love with Iason with Aphrodite's help (Pindar, *Pythian Odes* 4.213-219).

Ovid, *Metamorphoses* 4.167-273 tells the story of the love affair of Helios and Leukothoe.

The story of Cupid and Psyche is told by Apuleius, *Metamorphoses* 4.28-6.24. I have followed Apuleius closely, but to shorten the narrative I have omitted some details that could be predicted from many folklore analogues, notably the jealousy and punishment of Psyche's sisters and the first two of the three tasks set for Psyche by Venus. Apollo's oracle, quoted on p. 50, is from chapter 4.33. For the gems depicting Eros and Psyche see Faraone 1999 p. 45.

Chapter 4: The Story of Adonis

For 'Inanna's Descent to the Nether World', told here in brief, see the translation in Pritchard 1969 pp. 52-57. How the Kurgarru and

Galaturru persuade Ereshkigal to give them the body of Inanna is not clear from the fragmentary surviving text; the version given here draws on the conjectural reconstruction in Wolkstein and Kramer 1983 pp. 52-73. For the Akkadian version of the myth see 'The Descent of Ishtar to the Underworld' as translated in Pritchard 1969 pp. 106-109 and in Dalley 1989 pp. 154-162. On the worship offered to these gods by the Israelites in exile see Ezekiel 8.14; Jeremiah 44.15-19.

The famous story of Pygmalion and Galateia is told by Ovid, *Metamorphoses* 10.243-297. See also Apollodoros, *Library* 2.14.3; Arnobius, *Against the Gentiles* 6.22. George Bernard Shaw signalled the analogy between this tale and his own 'romance' of Liza Doolittle and Professor Higgins by choosing the title *Pygmalion* for his play.

For Aphrodite's possible anger with Smyrna see Apollodoros, *Library* 3.14.4; Hyginus, *Fables* 58. The story of Smyrna is told by Ovid, *Metamorphoses* 10.298-532; see also Apollodoros, *Library* 3.14.4; Antoninus Liberalis, *Metamorphoses* 34; Hyginus, *Fables* 58. For the fate of Smyrna, the origin of the myrrh tree and the birth of Adonis see *Scholia on Theokritos* 1.107; Ovid, *Metamorphoses* 10.476-532; Antoninus Liberalis, *Metamorphoses* 34; Apollodoros, *Library* 3.14.4 with Frazer's footnote; Hyginus, *Fables* 58, 164.

The story of Aphrodite and Adonis is mentioned briefly by Theokritos, *Idylls* 3.46-48 and told in full by Ovid, *Metamorphoses* 10.503-739. For their conversational exchanges I have often taken clues from Shakespeare's poem *Venus and Adonis*. See also Bion, *Lament for Adonis*. On the adjudication over Adonis see Apollodoros, *Library* 3.14.4; Nonnos, *Dionysiaka* 13.432-463. Some sources say that Zeus asked Kalliope to adjudicate and she gave each goddess six months with him (*Scholia on Theokritos* 3.48; Hyginus, *Astronomy* 2.6-7). Euboulos's play *Astytoi*, quoted in *Epitome of Athenaios* 69c-d, said that Aphrodite attended his funeral. On the lament for Adonis see Sappho fragment 140 Lobel and Page. Some claimed that Adonis was also the father of the phallic god Priapos (Apollonios of Rhodes 4.914-919; Diodoros of Sicily 4.83).

It is Ovid (*Metamorphoses* 10.560-680) who makes Aphrodite tell Adonis the story of Hippomenes and Atalanta. For some of the many variants of this story see Apollodoros, *Library* 3.9.2; Hesiod, *Catalogue of Women* fragments 72-76; Theokritos, *Idylls* 3.40-43; Philetas 18 Powell [*Scholia on Theokritos* 2.120]; Servius, *Commentary on Vergil's Aeneid* 3.113; Hyginus, *Fables* 185; Pliny, *Natural History* 8.43. Ovid, unlike earlier sources, makes the apples golden; I have not followed him in this detail. Some call Atalanta's successful suitor Melanion instead of Hippomenes.

Chapter 5: The Events on Mount Ida

The love affair of Aphrodite and Anchises is the main story of the *Homeric Hymn to Aphrodite*, from which the direct quotations in the text are taken. See also *Iliad* 2.819-821, 5.311-313; Hesiod, *Theogony* 1008-1010; Hyginus, *Fables* 94. The stories of Ganymede and Tithonos are told by Aphrodite to Anchises in the *Hymn* (for Tithonos see also *Iliad* 11.1, 20.237; Hesiod, *Theogony* 984-985). She does not explain clearly why she tells them. The answer given in the text – that they show why Anchises was right not to ask for immortality, because it is a two-edged gift to mortals – is suggested by Peter Smith's commentary on the *Hymn*. Tithonos is said in the *Iliad* to be the brother of Priam, king of Troy.

The author of the *Hymn* knew that Anchises was crippled as punishment for making love to an immortal, and in the *Hymn* Anchises himself foresees it; why, then, does Aphrodite promise him that it will not happen? The *Hymn* offers a possible solution to this self-created problem by making her afterwards demand that he keep their affair secret. Later sources assume, though the *Hymn* does not say, that he gave the secret away and was crippled as punishment for this.

Concerning apples as symbols of love see Pherekydes 3 F 17 Jakoby; Apollodoros, *Library* 2.5.11; Aristophanes, *Clouds* 996-997 with scholia; Faraone 1999 pp. 69-78.

The famous episode of the Judgement of Paris is narrated most fully by Lucian, *Dialogues of the Gods* 20, and then in the seventeenth century by Charles Coypeau d'Assoucy, *Le Jugement de Paris*; both authors are aiming for laughs. See also Euripides, *Troades* 919-937,

Andromache 274-300, *Iphigeneia at Aulis* 1283-1318; Isokrates, *Helen* 41-44; Ovid, *Art of Love* 1.247-248; Apollodoros, *Epitome* 3.2; Hyginus, *Fables* 92.

The description of Aphrodite's toilette is quoted from *Kypria* 5 West [Athenaios 682d] with acknowledgments to West's translation; see also Eustathios, *Commentary on Iliad* p. 979 line 61. Coypeau d'Assoucy likes to think that Aphrodite's preparations included trimming her pubic hair. *Iliad* 14.188-223 tells of the time when Hera borrowed the *kestos himas* from Aphrodite.

For Paris's return to Troy and expedition to Sparta see *Iliad* 5.59-64; *Scholia on Iliad* D 3.443 [= *Kypria* fragment 8 West]; *Scholia on Nikandros, Theriaka* 268; Apollodoros, *Epitome* 3.2; Hyginus, *Fables* 91. There is another story that Paris was in competition with his brother Deiphobos for the love of a boy named Antheus, son of Antenor; Paris accidentally killed the boy and then fled to Sparta (Lykophron, *Alexandra* 134 with scholia). On Helen's parentage see *Kypria* fragment 10 West [Athenaios 334b]; Apollodoros, *Library* 3.10.7.

On Menelaos's journey to Crete see Apollodoros, *Library* 3.2.1-2, *Epitome* 3.3; Diodoros of Sicily 5.59.1-4; Tzetzes, *Antehomerica* 96-134. The relationship between Paris and Helen, and their elopement, are narrated by *Iliad* 3.385-388; *Odyssey* 4.12-14; *Kypria* fragment 12 *PEG* and Proklos's summary; Ovid, *Art of Love* 2.359-372; Apollodoros, *Epitome* 3.3-4. The *Lakainai*, 'women of Sparta', who formed the chorus of a lost play by Sophokles, were probably Helen's maids, all of whom, for the dramatic purposes of that play, were with her at Troy. For the lovemaking on Kranae see *Iliad* 3.443-445; Pausanias 3.22.1; Strabon 9.1.22; Lykophron, *Alexandra* 110-111. Other events of the voyage are mentioned in Dictys Cretensis 1.5; *Iliad* 6.289-292; Proklos, *Chrestomathy*; *Kypria* fragment 14 West quoted by Herodotos 2.117. The lines on Aphrodite and the Nymphs and Charites are from *Kypria* fragment 6 West [Athenaios 682e] with acknowledgments to West's translation. The setting is certainly Ida, but whether the occasion is really Paris's wedding is unknown.

The advice about wine is from *Kypria* fragment 18 West [*Epitome of Athenaios* 35c]. It is West's suggestion to attribute these lines to Nestor.

For the abortive expedition that landed in Teuthrania and was driven back, see Pindar, *Olympian Odes* 9.70; Strabon, *Geography* 1.1.17; Proklos, *Chrestomathy*. For Oinone's asistance to the Greeks see Conon, *Narrations* 22; Tzetzes, *Scholia on Lykophron* 57 ff.

Chapter 6: The Fall of Troy and the Origin of Rome

The duel between Paris and Menelaos is a theme of *Iliad* book 3; the lines quoted are from *Iliad* 3.395-417. The prowess of Diomedes is the theme of *Iliad* book 5; for the wounding of Aphrodite and its aftermath see lines 311-430. The fighting of the Olympians before Troy is narrated at *Iliad* 21.391-433. The death of Paris, rejected by his unforgiving former wife Oinone, is told by Quintus of Smyrna, *After Homer* 10.253-489.

For the revisionist story of Helen see Stesichoros fragment 192-193 *PMG*; Plato, *Republic* 586c, *Phaidros* 243ab; Isokrates, *Helen* 64; Pausanias 3.19.13; Herodotos 2.112-120; Philostratos, *Life of Apollonios of Tyana* 4.16; Euripides, *Troades*, *Helen*, *Elektra*; Apollodoros, *Epitome* 3.5.

For Odysseus's reconnaissance and Helen's meeting with him see the *Little Iliad* as summarized by Proklos, *Chrestomathy*, cf. Aristotle, *Poetics* 1459b6; *Odyssey* 4.242-264; Apollodoros, *Epitome* 5.13; Aristophanes, *Wasps* 350-351; Antisthenes, *Aias* 6; Lykophron, *Alexandra* 779-785. For the purposes of Euripides's play *Hekabe* (lines 239-250), Helen identified Odysseus to queen Hekabe; however, he managed to persuade Hekabe to let him return to the Greek camp. According to Roman legend, Odysseus did not get the real *Palladion* but a copy: Aineias had the real image with him on his wanderings.

According to Vergil (*Aeneid* 6.494-534) Aeneas found out what happened to Deiphobos when he met Deiphobos's ghost in the Underworld. The reconciliation of Helen and Menelaos and her return to Sparta are told by Quintus of Smyrna, *After Homer* 13.385-415, 14.39-70, 14.149-178; see also *Odyssey* book 4. On the cup at Rhodes see Pliny, *Natural History* 33.81.

For the rescue of Aineias by Poseidon see *Iliad* 20.156-352.

Aphrodite's prediction that he would rule the Trojans is *Homeric Hymn to Aphrodite* 196-197. For the Greek versions of Aeneas's adventures on Troy's last day see Arktinos, *Capture of Troy* as summarized by Proklos, *Chrestomathy*; Sophokles fragment 373 Radt; Xenophon, *Hunting* 1.15; Apollodoros, *Epitome* 5.21; Lykophron, *Alexandra* 1261-1269 with scholia; Diodoros of Sicily 7.4; Aelian, *Miscellany* 3.22; Quintus of Smyrna, *After Homer* 13.315-327. In Vergil's version in *Aeneid* book 2, Aeneas himself is the narrator of the events. For the Greek versions of Aeneas's wanderings see Dionysios of Halikarnasos, *Roman Antiquities* 1.46-64, a long narrative based at least partly on Hellanikos. A first Roman version was apparently outlined by the early Latin poet Naevius, but his work is lost. In its fullest from the Aeneas story appears in Vergil's *Aeneid*. The love affair of Dido and Aeneas and the suicide of Dido are the theme of book 4.

The apotheosis of Aeneas is told by Ovid, *Metamorphoses* 14.581-608; for the discussion between Venus and Jupiter at the moment of Caesar's assassination see Ovid, *Metamorphoses* 15.760-860. The quotation about the 'long-haired star' or comet that signalled the apotheosis of Caesar is taken from Suetonius, *Life of Julius* 88.

Chapter 7: The Goddess of Love

The quotation about Venus's presence in Rome is from Ovid, *Art of Love* 1.57-60.

On the nature of Venus note Ovid, *Art of Love* 1.1-40, 2.397-424, 2.467-488, *Amores* 1.3, 1.4.67-68, 1.5.11-12; Lucretius, *On the Nature of the Universe* 1.1-49. On the word Venus see Simon 1990 p. 214; Alfred Ernout and Antoine Meillet, *Dictionnaire étymologique de la langue latine* (Paris: Klincksieck, 1985). For writers' prayers to Venus see Ovid, *Art of Love* 1.1-40, 3.43-56, 3.769-770; Lucretius, *On the Nature of the Universe* 1.1-49. On her temples see Livy 10.31.9, 22.10.9-10; Ovid, *Art of Love* 2.420, *Fasti* 4.863-886.

Eryx and Erykine are mentioned by Herodotos, *Histories* 5.43-46; Diodoros of Sicily 4.83; Cicero, *Against Caecilius* 55, *Against Verres* oration 3. The rock of Eryx, topped by the temple of Aphrodite, is depicted on Roman coins. On Eryx as son of Aphrodite see Apollodoros, *Library* 1.9.25; Apollonios of Rhodes 4.912-919; Diodoros of Sicily 4.83.1; *Orphic Argonautika* 1270-1297; Hyginus, *Fables* 14.

On the nature of Aphrodite see *Iliad* 14.347; Hesiod, *Theogony* 194, 971 with West's commentary; *Homeric Hymn to Aphrodite* 33-52; Aischylos, *Danaides* fragment 44 Radt; Euripides, *Hippolytos* 1420-1422. *Philommeides* is a difficult word; most translators stay with 'laughter-loving' but some have argued for 'lover of the genitalia'.

Among myths and legends in which Aphrodite plays a subsidiary part, note her assistance to Zeus in the making of Pandora (Hesiod, *Works and Days* 65-74); her patronage of Theseus (Plutarch, *Theseus* 18); her involvement with Medeia (Pindar, *Pythian Odes* 4.213-219; Apollonios of Rhodes, *Argonautika*; Graves 1955 chapter 152). Her anger with the Propoitides of Amathous (Ovid, *Metamorphoses* 10.220-242); with the Kerastai (Ovid, *Metamorphoses* 10.220-242, cf. 7.363-4); with the Lemnian women (Herodotos 6.138; Aischylos, fragments; Sophokles, fragments; Apollonios of Rhodes, *Argonautika* 1.607 ff. with scholia; Apostolius 10.65; Zenobius 4.91; *Orphic Argonautika* 473; *Scholia on Iliad* 7.468; Valerius Flaccus, *Argonautica* 2.77; Hyginus, *Fables* 15; Philostratos, *Heroika* 20.24); with Hippolytos (Euripides, *Hippolytos*; Pausanias 2.31.6; Ovid, *Heroides* 4.67) and the daughters of Acheloos (Graves 1955 chapter 170). Her kindness to the orphaned daughters of Pandareos (*Odyssey* 20.67-78; Pausanias 10.30.1; *Scholia on Odyssey* 19.518; Antoninus Liberalis, *Metamorphoses* 36); and to the ferryman Phaon (Palaiphatos 48; Aelian, *Miscellany* 12.15; Servius, *Commentary on Vergil's Aeneid* 3.279; *Epitome of Athenaios* 69d citing Kratinos).

The prayer by Sappho is Sappho fragment 1 quoted by Dionysios of Halikarnasos, *Composition* 23.

For the magic of Aphrodite see *Supplementum Magicum* no. 63 (translation after Faraone 1999); Herodotos, *Histories* 2.181; Euripides, *Hippolytos* 509-515. On the wryneck and other magical implements see Pindar, *Pythian Odes* 4.213-219; Aristophanes, *Lysistrata* 1110; Theokritos, *Idylls* 2.17; Xenophon, *Memorabilia* 3.11.17; *Anthologia Palatina* 5.205; cf. Vergil, *Eclogues* 8; Gow 1934; Faraone 1999.

On the temple of Aphrodite at Corinth see Pausanias 2.5.1. Both the temple and the statue of Aphrodite are depicted on Roman coins. On sacred prostitution at Corinth see Athenaios 573b-574c; Pindar, *Olympian Odes* 13. The quotation in the text is of Pindar fragment 107 Bowra [Athenaios 574a].

For Kythera see Pausanias, *Guide to Greece* 3.23.1; Herodotos, *Histories* 1.105. For Aphrodite at Paphos see Tacitus, *Histories* 2.2; Herodotos, *Histories* 1.105; Strabon, *Geography* 14.6.3.

For Inanna and Ishtar see Pritchard 1969, Dalley 1989 and Wolkstein and Kramer 1983; stories from all three collections appear in chapters 1 and 4 of this book. On Astarte there is some information from a Greek point of view in Lucian, *On the Syrian Goddess*.

All facts about Pythagoras are doubtful, including those in the text (for which the source is Diogenes Laertios, *Lives of the Philosophers*). The earliest surviving source for the name *Aphrodite's star* is Plato, *Epinomis* 987b; for *Venus* see Cicero, *Republic* 6.17. For *Inanna* as the Sumerian name of the planet see Wolkstein and Kramer 1983 pp. xvi, 123.

Further Reading

ON THE ORIGINAL SOURCES OF INFORMATION FOR MYTHS OF Aphrodite–Venus see 'Sources', pp. 135–46.

Ancient goddesses, modern representations

Caroline Arscott and Katie Scott, eds. *Manifestations of Venus: art and sexuality*. Manchester: Manchester University Press, 2000.

Stephanie Böhm, *Die 'nackte Göttin'*. Mainz: Philipp von Zabern, 1990.

Robert du Mesnil du Buisson, *Le sautoir d'Atargatis de la chaîne d'amulettes*. Leiden: Brill, 1947.

Paul Friedrich, *The meaning of Aphrodite*. Chicago: University of Chicago Press, 1978.

Geoffrey Grigson, *The goddess of love*. London: Constable, 1976.

Anthony Mortimer, *Variable passions: a reading of Shakespeare's Venus and Adonis*. New York: AMS Press, 2000.

Ishtar, Inanna and Near Eastern religion

Stephanie Dalley, tr. *Myths from Mesopotamia: Creation, The Flood, Gilgamesh and others*. Oxford: Oxford University Press, 1989.

Stephen Langdon, *Tammuz and Ishtar*. Oxford: Oxford University Press, 1914.

Betty De Shong Meador, tr. *Inanna, Lady of Largest Heart: poems of the high priestess Enheduanna*. Austin: University of Texas Press, 2000.

Simo Parpola, Julian Reade, eds. *Assyrian prophecies*. Helsinki: Helsinki University Press, 1997.

Diane Wolkstein and Samuel Noah Kramer, trs. *Inanna, queen of heaven and earth: her stories and hymns from Sumer*. New York: Harper and Row, 1983. London: Rider, 1984.

Aphrodite and Greek religion

Deborah Boedeker, *Aphrodite's entry into Greek epic*. Leiden: Brill, 1974.

L. R. Farnell, *The cults of the Greek states*. Oxford: Oxford University Press, 1896–1909.

James G. Frazer, tr. *Apollodorus: The library*. London, 1921. [Currently published by Harvard University Press.]

Timothy Gantz, *Early Greek myth: a guide to literary and artistic sources*. Baltimore: Johns Hopkins University Press, 1993.

Robert Graves, *The Greek myths*. Harmondsworth: Penguin, 1955.

Christine Mitchell Havelock, *The Aphrodite of Knidos and her successors: a historical review of the female nude in Greek art*. Ann Arbor: University of Michigan Press, 1995.

Vinciane Pirenne-Delforge, *L'Aphrodite grecque: contribution à l'étude de ses cultes et de sa personnalité dans le panthéon archaïque et classique*. Athens: Centre International d'Étude de la Religion Grecque Antique, 1994.

Erika Simon, *Die Götter der Griechen*. Munich: Hirmer, 1998.

Peter Smith, *Nursling of mortality: a study of the Homeric Hymn to Aphrodite*. Frankfurt am Main: Peter Lang, 1981.

T. C. W. Stinton, *Euripides and the Judgement of Paris*. London: Society for the Promotion of Hellenic Studies, 1965.

Martin L. West, ed. *Hesiod: Theogony*. Oxford: Oxford University Press, 1966.

Martin L. West, tr. *Greek epic fragments from the seventh to the fifth centuries BC*. Cambridge, Mass.: Harvard University Press, 2003.

Venus and Roman religion

James G. Frazer, tr. *Publii Ovidii Nasonis Fastorum libri sex*. London: Macmillan, 1929.

N. Horsfall, 'Some problems in the Aeneas legend' in *Classical Quarterly* vol. 29 (1979) pp. 372–90.

Erika Simon, *Die Götter der Römer*. Munich: Hirmer, 2001.

Index

A

Achilleus 108
Adonis 63, 67, 71–9, 122, 125, 131, 136
adultery 21, 34
Aegean Sea 22, 58, 97
Aeneas (Aineias) 87–9, 102–12, 115, 117, 129,
    130, 132, 135–6
Aesculapius 130
Agamemnon 95, 97–8, 101, 131–2
Aglaia 38
aigis see goatskin
Aineias see Aeneas
Ainos 34
Alba Longa 111, 112
alphabet 39
Amasis, king of Egypt 120
ambrosia 15, 17, 86, 111
Amor 49, 133, 135, see also Cupid, Eros
Amphitrite 15
An 79, 118, 122
Anchises 81–8, 92, 104, 108, 112, 131–2, 134, 135
Andromache 91
Anna 111
Apate 47
Aphrodite 11, 12, 31, 38, 67, 82, 91, 96, 118–24,
    132–4, see also Venus, *Homeric Hymn to
    Aphrodite*
Aphrodite Areia 38
Aphrodite kallipyge 118
Aphrodite pandemos 120
Aphrodite's star 85, 126
Apollo 14–17, 23, 27, 32–6, 50, 60, 75, 84, 104,
    130

Apollodoros 135, 136
apples 12, 66, 76, 89–90, 92, 94, 122
Apuleius 49, 125, 138
Arabia 48–9, 71
Ares 15–18, 23–39, 43–4, 47–8, 78, 89, 93, 104–6,
    125, 130, 131, see also Mars
Ariadne 24
Artemis 14–18, 40, 77–8, 84, 130, see also Diana
Ashtaroth 122
Askanios 108, 132, see also Iulus
Asklepios 130
Assyria 121–2
Astarte 122–3
Atalanta 75–7
Athene 14–15, 27, 38, 43, 55–8, 89–93, 101–9,
    130
Athens 118, 133
Augustus, Roman emperor 112, 115, 120, 130, 135
Aulis 98

B

Baal 48
Babylon 122
Bacchus 24, 130, see also Dionysos
balsam of Mecca 60
banquet for the Twelve Gods 117
Belili 67
Belos 48
Boutes 117
Bouthroton 109
Briareos 10
brooch, Venus's 21, 83, 85
Butrint 109

C

Cadmus see Kadmos
Caesar, G. Julius 112, 115, 120, 125, 130, 132
Caria 45, 133
Carthage 110–11, 117
Castor see Kastor
Cenchreis 69
Centaurs 89, 133
Cerberus 56, 57, 133
Ceres 53, 70, 71, 130, see also Demeter
Charis 38
Charites (Graces) 34–5, 59, 60, 83, 91, 96
Charon 56, 57
childbirth 53, 71
Cinyras see Kinyras
circlet, Venus's 12, 31, 83
Cleopatra see Kleopatra
Clytemnestra 132
coins 122, see also obol
comet ('long–haired star') 112, 115
Corinth 38, 46, 120, 121, 133
Coypeau d'Assoucy, Charles 125, 136
Crete 11, 96–7, 121, 133
Creusa see Kreousa
Cronos see Kronos
crown, Inanna's 12, 63, 64
Cupid (Cupido) 49–60, 69, 72–3, 110, 116, 124,
      125, 131, 133, 136, see also Eros
Cybele 76, 77, see also Mother of the Gods
Cyclopes see Kyklopes
Cypris see Kypris
Cyprus 11–12, 67–70, 76, 82–3, 96, 118, 121–2
Cyrene see Kyrene
Cythera see Kythera
Cytherea see Kythereia

D

Dardanos 85, 108, 131
Deimos 39, 131
Deiphobos 94, 107, 109
Delphi 16
Demeter 14, 33, 53, 130, see also Ceres
Demodokos 35
Diana 45, 74, 77, 130, see also Artemis
Dido 110–11
Didyma 50
Diodoros of Sicily 44
Diomedes 38, 103–8

Dione 9–10, 47, 104–5, 131
Dionysos 24–6, 39, 46, 130, 131
Don, river 29
Doris 9, 131
doves 13, 14
dowry 34, 36
Dryope 16
Dumuzi 63, 66–7, 79

E

Ea 66, 67
earrings, Venus's 13, 83, 85
Egypt 106–7, 112, 120–22, 125
Elektra 131
embroidered band (kestos himas) 13, 34, 63, 91,
      93, 137
Enki 12, 64–5
Enkimdu 63
Enlil 64–5
Enyalios 38
Eos 39–40, 86–7, 130
Epicurus 116
Epimenides 10–11
Erebos 47
Erech 12, 122
Ereshkigal 63–7
Erichthonios 43, 131
Erinyes (Furies) 10–11
Eris 39, 89–90
Eros 13, 47–9, 81–2, 88, 96–7, 106, 124, 131, 133,
      see also Cupid
Erykine (Erycina) 117
Eryx 117–18
Ethiopians 18
Etna, mount 24
Euphrates, river 12
Euripides 91, 118
Eurynome 21, 48

F

Fabius Maximus Cunctator, Q. 117
Fates 10, 79, 88
foam–born 9, 11, 118
Furies 10–11

G

Gaia (Gaea) 9–11, 43, 47, 71, 89, 130
Galatea 69, 72
Galaturru 65
Ganymedes (Ganymede) 86, 92, 104, 131, 133
Gargaros, mount 90, 92, 115
gens Iulia 112, 132
Gigantes (Giants) 11
Gilgamesh 12
goatskin, Athene's 15, 93, 105
Graces (Charites) 34–5, 38, 59, 60, 83, 91, 96
Greeks 97, 98, 103, 105, 108–9, 121, 125
Gyes 10

H

Hades 130
Halley's comet ('long–haired star') 112, 115
Harmonia 39, 131
Harpyes 47
Hekabe (Hecuba) 90, 94–5
Hektor 131
Helen 88–9, 94–8, 101–3, 106–9, 131–3
Helios 30–32, 35, 39, 43, 48–9, 88, 101, 130, see
    also Sun
Hellanikos 109
Heosphoros 125
Hephaistos 21–38, 43–4, 78, 81, 130–1, 136, see
    also Vulcan
Hera 14, 17, 21–5, 46, 81, 88–93, 105–6, 110, 130,
    131, see also Juno
Herakles (Hercules) 130
Hermaphroditos (Hermaphroditus) 44–5, 47, 131
Hermes 16–17, 23–4, 27, 33–4, 36, 44, 47, 84, 90,
    92, 107, 130–1, see also Mercury
Hermione 96
Herophilos 43, 131
Hesiod 13, 38, 40, 125, 133
Hesperos 125
Hestia 14, 130
Hippolytos 118
Hippomenes 75–7
Homer 133, 135, see also Iliad, Odyssey
Homeric Hymn to Aphrodite 81, 82, 85, 135
Homeric Hymn to Apollo 38
Horai (Horae) 13, 24, 58, 59, 91
hunting 72–9
Hyperboreans 40
Hyperion 130

I

Ida, mount 45, 81–4, 87, 90–98, 102, 108, 131,
    133
Iliad 15, 35, 38, 105, 106, 133, 135
Ilos 131, 132
immortality 71, 86–7
Inanna 12–13, 63–6, 89, 122, 136
Inanna, planet 126
Indiges 112
Iolkos 89
Iris 47, 97
Ishtar 13, 66–7, 122, 126, 136
Isis 122
Israelites 67
Iulus 110, 112, 132, see also Askanios
iynx 120

J

Jesus 71
Judgement of Paris 89–94
Juno 53, 110–11, 130, see also Hera
Jupiter 58–9, 111–12, 115, 130, see also Zeus

K

Kabeiroi 22, 130
Kadmos 39
Kaikos 97
Kassandra 94–5, 131–2
Kastor 95, 132
Katreus 96
Kephalos 40
Kerberos see Cerberus
kestos himas see embroidered band
Kinyras (Cinyras) 67–70, 122
Kleitos 40
Kleopatra 120
Klytaimestra 132
Klytie 49
Knidos 118, 119
Kore 130, see also Persephone, Proserpina
Korinthos see Corinth
Korythos 98
Kottos 10
Kranae 96, 103
Kreousa 131, 132
Kronos 10–11, 14, 130

Kurgarru 65
Kyklopes 10
Kypria 91, 96, 135
Kypris (*Cypris*) 11–12, 119, 121
Kyprogenes 11
Kypselos 38
Kyrene 119
Kythera (Cythera) 11, 76, 121
Kythereia (*Cytherea*) 11, 12, 121

L

Ladike 119
Lakedaimon see Sparta
Lampsakos 46
Laokoon 108
Laomedon 131, 132
lapis lazuli 12, 63, 64
Leda 88–9, 95, 132
Lemnos 22, 24, 28, 30, 31
leopards 76
Lesbos 97, 115, 119
Leto 83
Leukothoe 48–9
Lindos 108
lions 74, 76, 77
Lucian 125, 133, 136
Lucina 71
Lucretius 116
Lyros 132

M

Maia 16, 23
Mainads 24–8, 133
Mark Antony 120
Mars 116–17, 132, see also Ares
Mars, planet 39
Marsyas 16
Mary 124
me 12
Meliai 11
Menelaos 94–7, 101–3, 106–7, 109, 132
Mercury (Mercurius) 44, 59, 123, 130, see also
    Hermes
Mesopotamia 12, 63, 67, 122, 136
Minerva see Athene
Minoans 11, 121
Minos 96

Moirai (Fates) 10, 79, 88
Mother of the Gods 122, see also Cybele
Muses 16, 60
Mycenae (Mykenai) 95, 97, 133
myrrh 71, 135

N

Nanna 64, 65
necklace, Venus's 13, 63–4, 85
nectar 15, 37, 86, 91, 111
Nemesis 95, 132
Neptune (Neptunus) 58–9, 130, see also Poseidon
Nereids 9, 129, 131
Nereus 9, 15, 130, 131
Nestor 97
net, Hephaistos's 32–4
Neti 64
New Year 66–7, 122
Ninshubur 64–6
Numicius 111
Nymphs 87, 96–7, 129, see also Meliai, Nereids,
    Okeanids
Nyx 47

O

obol 56, 57
Ocean (Okeanos) 9, 10, 21, 71, 86–7, 91, 129
Odyssey 35, 125, 133, 135
oil 35, 51–3, 57, 83
Oinone 92, 98, 107
Okeanids 9
Okeanos see Ocean
Olympia 38, 121
Olympos, Mount 14–6, 21–34, 39–40, 46, 56, 88,
    91, 103–4, 129–31
Opis 40
oracles 16, 50, 75, 122
Orchamos 48–9
Orion 40
Orpheus 74
Osiris 122
Otreus 84
Ourania 121
Ouranos (Uranus) 9–11, 47, 130
Ovid 44, 67, 69–71, 74, 77, 115–17, 124–5, 133,
    135

P

Palestine 122–3
Palladion 107
Pandaros 104
Paphia 12, 121
Paphos 11–12, 34, 67, 69, 83, 121–2
Papsukkal 66–7
Paris 89–109, 112, 125, 131–2, 135–6
Pausanias 38, 121
pearls 22, 63
Peitho 46–7, 131
Peleus 89, 129
pendant, Venus's 64, 95
Persephone (Proserpina) 55–7, 78–9, 130
Persians 120
Phaethon 40
Phaon 118
Phobos 38–9, 131
Phoenicia 39, 48, 96, 110, 121, 133
Phosphoros 125
Photios 135
Phrygia 84
Pindar 46, 120–21, 133
Pleiades 131
Plutarch 133
Pluto 130
polenta 56–7
Polydeukes (Pollux) 95, 132
Pontos 10, 130
Poseidon 15–17, 23, 27, 33–8, 43–4, 108, 130,
    131, see also Neptune
Praxiteles 119
Priam 90, 94–7, 107, 109, 131–3
Priapos 46–47, 131
Proklos 135
Proserpina (Persephone) 55–7, 78–9, 130
prostitution 46, 53, 67, 79, 117, 120–23
Proteus 106
Psyche 50–60, 64, 69, 125, 136
purple 68
Pygmalion 67–8, 74
Pylos 97, 121
Pythagoras 126

R

Remus 112
Rhea 14, 130
Rhodes 43, 45, 108, 133

Rhodos 43, 131
Rome 49, 53, 101, 110–17, 132, 133, 136
Romulus 112

S

Salmacis (Salmakis) 45
Samothrake 22, 24, 130
sandals 21, 31
Sappho 46–7, 119
Saturnus 132
Satyrs 24, 25, 129, 131, 133
Scythia 29, 133
sea 9, 11, 13, 15, 21, 89
seashells 9, 11, 68, 83, 85
Seasons see Horai
Seilenos 24–6, 130
Selene 132
Semele 24, 39, 46
Shakespeare, William 73, 74, 125, 136
Sicily 117
Sidon 96
Silenus see Seilenos
Simonides 47
Sintians 30, 31
Sleep 58
Smyrna 67, 69–71, 74, 135
snakes 11, 16
Socotra 71
Sollicitudo 54
Somalia 71
sparrows 13, 14, 34, 119
Sparta 38, 55, 89, 94–5, 103, 108, 132, 133
Stesichoros 106
Sthenelos 104
stoning 49
Stromboli 24
Styx, river 56, 57
Suetonius Tranquillus, C. 112, 115
Sumerians 12, 63, 66, 89, 122, 125–6
sun 28–30, 32, 35–9, 43, 49, 63, 66, see also Helios
swans 14, 77
symbols, gods as 124

T

Taenarum (Tainaros) 55, 57–9, 133
Tamasus 76
Tammuz 63, 66–7, 79, 131

Tanais 29
Tartaros 14
Tegea 29, 35
Telephos 97
Tethys 91
Teuthrania 97
Thebes 39, 133
Themis 83, 89
Theoklymenos 106
Theokritos 79
Theseus 118
Thetis 21–2, 89, 129, 131
Thrace 34, 133
throne, Hera's 22–5
Timaios 109
Titans 9, 10, 130
Tithonos 40, 86
Titus, Roman emperor 122
Tristities 54
triton–shell 12
Trojan War 38, 88–9, 97–109, 131, 135, see also Troy and Trojans
Tros 86, 104, 131
Troy and Trojans 45, 82, 84, 86, 88, 90, 94–112, 129, 131–3, 136, see also Trojan War
Tyndareos 89, 95, 132

U

Underworld 14, 55–7, 63–6, 78–9, 84, 129, 130
Uranus see Ouranos
Uruk 66
Utu 63, 66

V

Venus passim; origin and birth 9–13; entry to Mount Olympos 13–18; marriage 26–36; affairs with Ares and others 28–47, with Adonis 72–9, with Anchises 81–8; at the Judgement of Paris 89–94; in the Trojan War 102–6; children 43–8, 86–9, 102–12; descendants 108–15
Venus Erycina 117
Venus, planet 85, 125–6
Vergil 108–11, 124, 133, 135–6
Vesta see Hestia
Vinalia rustica 117
Voluptas 60
Vulcan (Vulcanus) 59, 130, see also Hephaistos

W

wand, Inanna's 64
weddings 39, 50–51, 60, 69, 89–90, 96–8, 110
wine 24–5
Wooden Horse 107–8
wreath, Venus's 13
wryneck 120

X

Xenophon of Corinth 121

Z

Zelos 47
Zephyros 47
Zeus 9–10, 13–17, 21–7, 32–9, 44–7, 78–81, 85–95, 101, 104–5, 119, 130–2, see also Jupiter